Culture
Myths

Applying Second
Language Research
to Classroom Teaching

Andrea DeCapua, Ed.D.

University of Michigan Press
Ann Arbor

ISBN-13: 978-0-472-03723-0

2021   2020   2019   2018   4   3   2   1

Contents

Acknowledgments

In my more than 30 years of teaching, there have been many students and workshop participants whose comments, journals, blogs, discussion board comments, essays, and class and private conversations provided rich material *Culture Myths*. In the interest of privacy, when I have used any of these materials, I have used pseudonyms. One exception is Amira, who specifically requested that I use her first name.

I would also especially like to thank the following colleagues for sharing their stories and insights with me: Kenneth Kuo-Pin, lecturer, Fu Jen Catholic University, Taipei, Taiwan; Shawna Shapiro, assistant professor, Middlebury College, Middlebury, Vermont; and Camilla Vásquez, professor, University of South Florida, Tampa, Florida. I also thank Ümit from Turkey who asked I use only the first name. Finally, special thanks to Helaine W. Marshall, professor, Long Island University–Hudson (Purchase, New York), for her review of and suggestions for Myths 6 and 7.

I also gratefully acknowledge the support and help of my wonderful editor, Kelly Sippell.

Introduction

Culture is communication and communication is culture.

(Hall, 1984, p. 169)

Culture Myths is intended for all educators who work with culturally and linguistically diverse students of any age and at any level. The intention of the title is to convey the idea that one group of people holds culturally derived beliefs and makes assumptions about another group of people who holds diverse beliefs and assumptions; each group's assumptions are formed in different cultural contexts.

This book does not teach U.S. values, beliefs, and norms. Rather, it seeks to develop readers' appreciation for and deeper understanding of what culture is and how culture impacts how we think and behave, particularly as it relates to teaching and learning. The book's focus is on some of the more common myths about culture that U.S. educators encounter routinely, what the research tells us about these myths, and what we can do to address them.

We live in an increasingly global society where we encounter and interact with members of different cultures on a daily basis. Cultural differences are what lie at the heart of the tendency to evaluate members of other cultures negatively (Peeples, Hall, & Seiter, 2012). One goal of this book is to develop cross-cultural awareness to minimize this tendency, or at the very least, encourage readers to recognize this very real predisposition to frame judgments of others through our own cultural lens or cultural assumptions. Cultural assumptions can be thought of as a type of *implicit bias*, a term often used when discussing race and gender to refer to the unconscious attitudes, stereotypes, and preconceptions that influence interpretations of, behaviors toward, and decisions about those who are different than ourselves (Banaji & Greenwald,

2013). Implicit bias is most likely an evolutionary artifact of safety needs and appears to be rooted in a basic human tendency to see people in terms of groups—that is, "us versus them" or "in-group versus out-group" (Cikara & Van Bevel, 2014). This tendency, however, can be overcome through deliberate reflection, exploration, and examination (Yudkin et al., 2016).

This book does not propose to judge or change, but to create and develop an understanding of how complex the idea of "culture" truly is. It is designed to help readers observe, evaluate, and appreciate cultural differences in values, beliefs, behaviors, attitudes, and worldviews by focusing on underlying and mostly invisible reasons for these differences. By developing an awareness of our own cultural assumptions, we can better overcome cultural barriers and stumbling blocks to communication and understanding, both in the classroom and in the world outside the classroom.

Fundamental to developing cross-cultural awareness is learning about and understanding one's own culture, values, and beliefs and how they impact one's worldview, identity, and behaviors. We don't necessarily know our own culture by simply being a member of a culture, as illustrated in this parable told by David Foster Wallace (2005):

> There are these two young fish swimming along, and they happen to meet an older fish swimming the other way, who nods at them and says, "Morning, boys. How's the water?" And the two young fish swim on for a bit, and then eventually one of them looks over at the other and says, "What the hell is water?"

Although misunderstandings across cultures cannot be avoided completely, we can learn to appreciate that there are differences and learn how to evaluate whether misunderstandings and miscommunications are based on cultural differences rather than personality

(Lanteigne, 2007). In so doing, we can learn to differentiate between what is "rude" and "inappropriate" and what may be culturally different ways of thinking or doing something. Learning to understand how and why cultures differ is very much a consciousness-raising endeavor. We cannot understand everything, yet we also do not only want to focus on cultural dos and taboos. By learning to observe and evaluate the words, behaviors, and actions of members of other cultures and one's own, we become aware of the role of culture in our lives. In so doing, however, we must strike a balance between minimizing cultural differences and assuming similarities across cultures versus exoticizing other cultures or accentuating surface dissimilarities. We must also realize that no culture is homogeneous or static and that culture consists of practices and processes that vary according to contexts and change over time.

Culture is more than a collection of readily observable facts or a menu of "dos and taboos in Country X or Country Y." A popular classroom activity is to use culture quizzes or lists from the internet. Although many of these culture quizzes or lists purport to reveal cultural differences and promote cultural understanding, they only superficially address what culture is and how it impacts our behaviors and worldviews. And, at worst, these types of culture quizzes or lists perpetuate implicit biases and stereotypes. Therefore, I caution readers to examine culture quizzes or lists carefully before using them as a teaching tool.

Introducing Key Concepts

Several key concepts, often referred to as *cultural constructs*, will be referred to throughout the book. Brief descriptions are given here, but more extensive explanations and examples appear in the chapter in which they are first introduced so that readers can better explore how these concepts underlie diverse attitudes and behaviors.

- **culture**

In *Culture Myths, culture* is used to mean identifiable cognitive patterns of behavior, including the shared practices, customs, values, beliefs, norms, experiences, and worldviews that a group of people use for understanding and engaging with the world around them (McDaniel, Samovar, & Porter, 2014; Nasir & Hand, 2006). This definition focuses on underlying and less apparent elements of culture rather than on the more visible ones of language, food, music, art, and dress that are often the more commonly understood examples of "culture" in mainstream society. See Myth 1.

- **collectivism / individualism**

Collectivism and *individualism* are broad terms that describe how members of cultures understand who they are in relationship to others. In *collectivistic* cultures, people primarily see themselves as part of an interconnecting, mutually dependent web of relationships or groups. In these cultures, people's actions and behaviors transpire and are evaluated within a context of how they will affect other members in this web, or the group, and the needs and wants of a person will often be subsumed to those of the group. In *individualistic* cultures, people primarily consider themselves to be independent units, and individual wants and desires dominate their conduct and choices. See Myth 2.

- **face**

Some readers may be familiar with this term and the concept it represents; *face* is how people maintain their dignity, self-esteem, and/or reputation in public contexts. While this definition is a good starting point, in Asian cultures, *face* is a concept that takes on a much deeper and more central role than it does in the Western world. When a person is embarrassed or shamed in front of others, from the Asian perspective, it reflects not only on that one individual, but also on every member of the larger group that that person identifies with—whether that group is the family, a kinship group, a country, or something else. Thus, the avoidance of behaviors and language that could potentially threaten both others and one's own face is considered essential. See Myth 2.

- **American**

In accordance with everyday usage, in this book I use the term *American* to refer specifically to the people who were born and live in the United States and to examples and information specific to the United States of America. Nevertheless, I am aware that all people from Central and South America are also Americans.

Organization of the Book

This book follows others in the University of Michigan Press series on myths on language learning and teaching. It also builds on my book, co-authored with Ann Wintergerst, *Crossing Cultures in the Language Classroom, Second Edition*. This book examines seven myths related to culture that affect teaching in the U.S. classroom. Readers should note that the content of each chapter connects to and intersects with information in other chapters—that is, the myths are not "mutually exclusive" because culture is complex and multifaceted. The aim is for readers to find connections and discover cultural patterns of other cultures and their own in order to develop cross-cultural awareness. The myths related to culture in the classroom are:

> Myth 1: We are all human beings, so how different
> can we really be?

> Myth 2: The goal of education is to develop each
> individual's potential.

> Myth 3: Focusing on conversational skills in the
> classroom is overrated.

> Myth 4: Not looking at the teacher shows disrespect.

Myth 5: How something is said is not as important as what is said.

Myth 6: Everyone knows what a good instructional environment is.

Myth 7: By the time students get to middle or high school, they know how to be a student.

Like the other books in the University of Michigan Press Myths series, I have adopted the same organization. Each chapter begins with stories or anecdotes from the real world to introduce the myth. This is followed by a look at some research that examines pertinent research related to the myth. The last section in each chapter offers suggestions on what teachers can do to promote cultural awareness related to the myth that is the focus of that chapter. The suggestions are based on the premise that teachers need to incorporate activities that actively engage learners in analyzing, interpreting, and reflecting on different elements of culture. In so doing, we develop an understanding of the *why* of culture and cultural differences—that is, the underlying reasons for such differences. The references for all chapters can be found at the end of the book.

A Note about Myths That Didn't Make It Into the Book

In preparing to write this book, I queried many colleagues and teachers as to what they thought were common cross-cultural myths. Many of their suggested myths, as valuable as they were, did not make it into this book. Generally, these suggestions fell into two categories. First, myths that could not be addressed because of a lack of sound or extensive research. For example, the myth "Immigrant parents don't care about education so they don't get involved in their children's schools" was mentioned several times.

While this is an important myth that deserves to be dispelled, it is not a chapter in its own right. For those interested in pursuing this myth, there is extensive research on the value of immigrant parental involvement in schools, reasons why immigrant parents might not participate, as well as evidence-based suggestions on how to encourage immigrant parental involvement (see, for example, Ordoñez-Jasis et al., 2016; Uy, 2015).

The second category of myths that did not make it into this book were those that have been extensively dealt with elsewhere. For instance, I received numerous suggestions for myths concerning second language writing. A single chapter would not have done any of these myths justice. Furthermore, there is an extensive body of research spanning more than five decades examining non-native speakers and the development of second language writing skills: see Casanave (2017) for a review and *Writing Myths* (Reid et al., 2008).

One more topic I would like mention is myths related to time. While there is an abundance of material on cross-cultural understandings of time, there are few research-based connections between time and school. After discussions with my editor and comments from outside reviewers, I made the decision to not include any myths related to the concept of time and to instead focus on integrating cross-cultural conceptualizations of time and teaching and learning into other myths where they best applied.

MYTH 1

We are all human beings, so how different can we really be?

In the Real World . . .

We all have some vague notion of what culture is, but what most of us don't have is a deep understanding of everything encompassed by this word. For some people, the initial reaction to the word *culture* is to think of art, music, dance, holidays, architecture, language, clothing, and food. However, we can conceptualize culture in two distinct ways: Culture written with a capital C and culture written with a lowercase c (Bennett, 1998). *Big C Culture* refers to those aspects of culture that first come to mind for many people—that is, music, dance, food, and so on. These aspects are easily observable and concrete. *Little c culture,* on the other hand, indicates cognitive elements, such as beliefs, norms, behaviors, and worldviews. These aspects are not as obvious because they are generally below the level of conscious awareness.

When teaching cross-cultural awareness workshops and classes, I typically begin by asking participants to share their first encounter with "little c culture," which is based on identifying cognitive processes of how a group of people think, behave, and view the world. Carla, a former student, once wrote:

> "Culture" as a term didn't mean much to me originally. I didn't consider myself "American—you know, a flag-waving, hot dog–eating, baseball-loving monolingual English speaker. I'd traveled a lot with my family. I'd studied Spanish in school. I ate all kinds of food from all over the world, went to lots of international festivals, loved foreign literature, music—considered myself a "person of the world." Then I studied abroad for a year in Ecuador, lived with a host family, and realized that I really was an American in ways I hadn't thought about before—in the ways I walked, thought, and acted. It was only when I realized that my new friends, "family," and teachers, although wonderful, caring people, often found me rude, inappropriate, cold, or whatever—not because I am that way but because I was doing things the "American" way and not the "Ecuadorian" way.

Another person, Yuta, responded this way:

> I always knew that I am Japanese, that my culture is Japanese and that means that many special things are different about us. But knowing this and then coming to study in U.S. was when I realized how very Japanese I am in ways I never thought about before. People here just do and think so many things different and in so many little ways I can't describe, but I feel and I see. Now I really know why I am "Japanese."

These two responses can illustrate how little we know about ourselves as persons shaped by our own socialization experiences. We may think we know who we are; we may even deny how much our culture has shaped who we are. It is only when we encounter situations where we experience real differences in behavior and thinking, and have opportunities to reflect and evaluate our experiences, that we realize just how much our culturally influenced prior learning experiences play a decisive role in who we are. Reflecting on and critically evaluating the influence of culture is not easy. Much of the difficulty in developing the ability to do so is derived from our predisposition to interpret the world based on our own experiences or enculturation, and not realizing the role of little c culture.

Enculturation is the process of children becoming adults who internalize the beliefs, values, behaviors, and worldviews of their cultural community (Hofstede, 1980). In this enculturation process, which largely takes place subconsciously, as illustrated by Carla's story, we learn to understand the world in culturally specific ways. To illustrate this, we can think of the Asian story of the elephant and the six blind men often retold in English:

> Each of the blind men touches a different part of an elephant as he tries to grasp what an elephant is. Based on what each blind man touches, each draws very different conclusions about what an elephant is. One blind man, for example, feels only the tusk. He concludes that an elephant is "like a spear." Another blind man feels the trunk. His conclusion is that an elephant is "like a snake." None of the six blind men is right because each one only knows what he "perceives"; likewise, our cultural knowledge is a result of our enculturation until we are confronted with diverse cultures that force us to re-examine our assumptions and worldviews.

But we still haven't defined culture. What is exactly little c culture? The consensus, despite the many and varied definitions generated over the years, is that culture refers to clearly identifiable cognitive patterns of behaviors, including language, customs, beliefs, values, systems of social organization and worldviews shared by a group of people (McDaniel, Samovar, & Porter, 2014; Nasir & Hand, 2006). Everyone is a member of a culture in that they share systematic ways of understanding and organizing the world around them with a group of people. The ways we behave, speak, and understand the world are shaped, like the six blind men, by our culturally influenced prior learning experiences and practices. This allows us to identify general cultural patterns, keeping in mind that (1) culture is not a "thing" but a system of cognitive processes reflected in practices (Shepard, 2014) and (2) no culture is homogeneous; there are subcultural differences within any culture as well as individual variations (Lewis, 2006; Purcell-Gates et al., 2014).

Because so much of culture is below the level of conscious awareness, we generally only see differences when we encounter instances of cultural confusion or misunderstandings. As teachers, it is important for us and our students to develop cross-cultural awareness by exploring and evaluating what cultural elements might underlie misconceptions (DeCapua & Wintergerst, 2016; Qin, 2014). *Cultural awareness* entails developing the ability to evaluate critically how people's behaviors, practices, attitudes, and worldviews derive from cultural values, beliefs, and norms (Byram, 1997, 2012). It means learning to reflect on our own culture and becoming more aware of how "normal" and "mundane" aspects of our own lives, including language use, are culturally situated. As we develop cultural awareness, we learn to observe, interpret, and analyze the behaviors of members to understand how these are manifestations of cognitive processes underlying cultural practices.

Ideally, we experience cultural variations and learn from them. However, what often happens is that we experience someone behaving differently and then judge: "Those _____. They can never do _____. It's no wonder that _____ ." I'm sure as you read these sentence frames, you can easily fill in the blanks with less than positive judgments. What so often happens is that we encounter someone doing something in a way that we find peculiar or unexpected and then filter that through our own cultural lenses, often assuming they are doing it "wrong" because we do it "right." We then tend to react, rather than evaluate rationally and, in so doing, interpret the behaviors and actions of others from our cultural point of view as illustrated by these types of sentence frames. If we take the time to evaluate more logically, we consider what the underlying reasons for another perspective or different behaviors might be. We can accept that behaviors and actions are not a matter of better or worse, suitable or lacking, rude or considerate, obsequious or polite, but that they vary for reasons that we may not be aware of. However, they can be understood through observation, reflection, inquiry, and analysis. When we do that, we avoid negative evaluations, overgeneralizations, and stereotypes.

We also need to recognize that culture is not static or fixed. Identifiable cultural patterns and practices vary according to contexts and change over time in response to events, outside influences, and the needs of the members of a culture (Angouri, 2010; McDaniel, Samovar, & Porter, 2014). What may have been more or less true twenty or thirty years ago may no longer hold true for urban residents, younger generations, students studying abroad, or working professionals, especially those working in global contexts. For example, Mainland China is a nation that has experienced significant cultural and societal change since the implementation in the late 1970s of the open-door policy. Prior to the open-door policy, China was almost completely isolated from contact with the Western world. Since then, with the greater contact between China and the West, indications are that younger generations are more likely to support individual relationships and family values in line with Western Anglo-European cultures than the collectivism and traditional values of older generations (Chen, 2015).

To take two other examples that illustrate cultural change: In 2015, more than 50 percent of South Korean youth reported that cohabitation before marriage was acceptable, a significant change in this traditionally conservative culture. Previously, such behavior would have brought shame to the families, particularly to those of the woman (Denny, 2015). Second, when McDonald's first opened in Hong Kong in 1975, people crowded and jostled each other around the registers to place their orders because standing in orderly lines was not a common practice. Gradually, local managers changed this free-for-all by hiring line monitors to promote standing in line. Although McDonald's did not introduce standing in line to Hong Kong, McDonald's is popularly credited with so encouraging orderly lines that, by the 1980s, this had become the norm and came to represent the new, cosmopolitan Hong Kong (Watson, 2006).

Are Culture and Ethnicity the Same?

A common mistake, exacerbated by the mainstream media, is to associate ethnicity with culture. *Ethnicity* refers to a large group of people who share linguistic, racial, national, cultural, or other characteristics. Ethnicity, as well as culture, may be tied to people's physical features and skin color, although this is not necessarily so. Another one of my students, Jon, who was an American of Korean descent, recounted how people assumed he was Chinese because of how he looked:

> We lived in a primarily white middle-class neighborhood. Most of my classmates growing up were of Italian, Irish, German, [or] European descent, with a few Asians from different countries sprinkled in. Those who didn't know us thought we were all just Chinese. That bothered me some growing up, but it was nothing I realized [compared to what happened] when I went on a university study abroad year to Scotland: I had people stop me on the street and ask me where a good Chinese restaurant was; university students approached me to practice their Chinese; and people turned around to stare at me when I went "off the beaten path." It didn't matter that I was American. To them I was Chinese.

Associating ethnicity with culture occurs globally. Another student, Takahashi, a first-generation American whose parents emigrated to the U.S. long before he was born, wrote:

> I speak Japanese fluently; my sister and I were raised bilingually. But I learned Japanese [in the U.S.] and never lived in Japan. As a result, I consciously refused to incorporate certain cultural elements of the Japanese language. When I was in 10th grade, I spent a month in a Japanese school in Tokyo. All the students in the higher grades demanded that I speak to them with more respect. I knew how to do this, but it seemed wrong because, for me, it went against who I am—an American where you earn respect through actions and aren't just given it because of your age. I got beat up more than once because of my "disrespect" but I never changed because it was who I was—someone who physically looks Japanese but who is culturally American.

The fact that how people look does not indicate their culture is vividly illustrated in Ken Tanaka's humorous and instructive YouTube video, "What Kind of Asian Are You?" In this video, two actors portray a white American man and a Japanese-American woman. The man encounters the woman on a jogging path, greets her, and can't accept that she's an American because she doesn't look like his notion of an American. Likewise, the famous Nigerian author Chimamanda Ngozi Adichie warns in her TED talk "The Danger of a Single Story" about seeing Africa as one country and one culture. Conflating the thousands of different cultures on the continent of Africa into one story leads to stereotyping and pigeonholing.

In addition to not equating ethnicity with culture, we must also be careful not to overgeneralize and assume that because a person comes from a specific culture, he or she will behave in a certain way and share a common language. As human beings, when we encounter others from a different culture, we tend to assume everyone in that culture is the same because we are outsiders and not attuned to subcultural differences. Another former student of mine, Lara, a bilingual Spanish-English teacher working on her Master's in TESOL, told the story of being asked to evaluate a child from Guatemala in her school. This sixth grader was making almost no progress, despite having been placed in the school's dual Spanish-English language program for almost five months. Consequently, there were concerns that the child was intellectually disabled. When Lara met with this student, it turned out that he was not a Spanish speaker but a native speaker of K'iche', one of the many indigenous languages of Guatemala. The only Spanish he knew was what he was currently learning in school. But, because he came from Guatemala, the assumption was that he was a native speaker of Spanish, the official and primary language of the country. Not only was this a language issue, it was also a cultural issue. The student was a member of an indigenous Mayan culture, which differs significantly from the dominant culture of Guatemala.

To summarize, in the real world three things happen regarding culture:

1. We jump to conclusions about a behavior that is different from ours and consider it "strange" or "wrong."
2. We often too quickly assign behaviors based on how someone looks (ethnicity).
3. We sometimes fail to respect individual differences by giving too much weight to culture in explaining behavior.

What the Research Says . . .

Most of culture is below our level of conscious awareness—that is, most of culture is little c culture, which is the abstract, invisible elements that shape people's behaviors and worldviews (DeCapua & McDonell, 2008). In Hall's words (1984), "Culture hides much more than it reveals, and strangely enough, what it hides, it hides most effectively from its own participants" (p. 29).

What are some of these hidden elements? They include values, beliefs, gender roles, attitudes toward aging, non-verbal communication, notions of self and the role of the individual, assumptions about teaching and learning, and many more. As humans we all have beliefs, we all communicate, we all age, we all learn, and we all have societal roles—we share these things. But we don't all share the same culture because the "hidden elements" derive from disparate cognitive processes formed through enculturation into one's culture; thus, members of diverse cultures view and understand and act on all these hidden elements in distinct ways.

To help conceptualize visible and hidden or invisible elements of culture, the metaphor of an iceberg is frequently used (Ting-Toomey & Chung, 2011). Like an iceberg, the visible elements of culture form the smaller tip that can be seen above the water, while, below the water lurk the hidden elements that are much more substantial; see Figure 1.1.

Time is an example of a hidden element of culture. On one hand, we all think we know what time is, but do we really? Is time an independent quantity that we can divide into increasingly smaller units, such as century, year, month, week, day, hour, minute, second, nanosecond? Or is time something that exists as a continuum that has meaning only as we experience it (Mangaliso, 2001)? As we explore the concept of time across cultures, we find that there are different conceptualizations of time, observable in

Figure 1.1: Iceberg Model of Culture

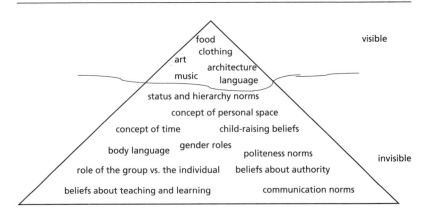

divergent cultural attitudes toward time (White, Valk, & Dialmy, 2011; Whitrow, 2004). Hall (1966, 1984), the groundbreaking U.S. anthropologist who studied the hidden elements of culture, argued that time is a "silent language." We cannot see "time" in the same way we can see physical manifestations of cultural differences, yet cultural conceptualizations and uses of time, the "silent language" of a culture, are fundamental in revealing much about a culture's values, norms, behaviors, and worldviews.

Hall distinguishes between two broad understandings of time, monochronic and polychronic. *Monochronic* cultures view time as linear—that is, as an independent quantity that can be divided up and that is therefore valuable. Monochronic time cultures like the U.S tend to regard time as an absolute or objective concept; it is something that *just is*. Members of monochronic cultures are very aware of time—time is a valuable commodity that must be planned and accounted for, well into the future. Because time is so precious, it must be "used" efficiently and should not be wasted. Planning calendars, schedules, appointments, and punctuality are all important when time is perceived as being linear and quantifiable—divisible into measurable, uniform, and valuable units.

Polychronic cultures, in contrast, conceive of time as flexible; lives are not rigidly governed by the clock and schedules are changeable because events, people, and relationships take priority. Many things can take place at the same time; doing tasks and accomplishing goals do not need to be done lockstep to fixed schedules. Time revolves around events rather than around the clock (Anderson & Venkatesan, 1994). Events govern the pace and tempo of how members of a culture live, think, and feel about time. Time is flexible, or, as is said in some Spanish-speaking cultures, *Hay más tiempo que vida* [There is more time in the world than there is life]. To emphasize the difference in the time perspective between polychronic and monochronic cultures, some researchers have labeled them clock-time cultures and event-time cultures (Lauer, 1981; Levine, 1997).

Cultures that are more event time–oriented are governed by a more flexible concept of time that emphasizes social time and family and community events such as weddings and festivals. I have had many teachers tell me over the years how they have had students absent for an extended period (from the U.S. perspective) for reasons such as weddings, festivals, and funerals. Students from the Dominican Republic, for instance, may leave at the beginning of winter break and not return to their schools in the U.S until mid-January. This is a time to be with friends and the extended family for the holidays, including celebrating Three Kings on January 6. In cultures like that of the Dominican Republic, collectivism and the centrality of the group is highly evident, and time and schedules are not perceived as superordinate or determining factors in people's behavior, including the timetable of school (Lambrev, 2015). It is not a question of the family or students not valuing education; their priority is the family and community and associated events over the U.S. school schedule.

Time Perceptions and School

How members of different cultures perceive time has educational ramifications that do not always align with those of the U.S. educational system.

In the U.S in Grades K–12, there are explicit rules and regulations governing attendance and procedures for lateness. Students who come late to school must stop at an office, provide a valid (often written) excuse, and then receive authorization to go to class. In addition, many schools at the secondary level signal the end and beginning of classes with a bell.

At the university level, punctuality is expected although there are no universitywide formal procedures for coming late to class, and it can sometimes be a challenge to get newly arrived international students to understand what "on time" means and what they should do when they come late to class. Arriving fifteen minutes late to university classes in some cultures is still "on time," whereas in the U.S., this is considered late. In many cultures, late students knock on the door, wait for the professor to open it, and then greet the professor and the rest of the class before taking a seat. In the U.S., such behavior is regarded as disruptive, and students arriving late are expected to minimize the interruption by discreetly opening the door (if closed) and taking a seat with, at most, a quietly uttered, "Sorry I'm late."

Because polychronic cultures regard people and relationships as having priority over time schedules, students and families from other cultures may have a different concept of personal relationships with teachers, administrators, and school personnel. In cultures, such as Latin American ones, that highly value personal relationships, small talk (see Myth 3) has an important function in fostering teacher-family relationships.

In parent-teacher conferences in the U.S., teachers are generally scheduling time slots and agendas that focus on student progress with minimal, if any time for "digressions," or small talk. Such tight planning and focus, from the teachers' perspective, allows them to meet with as many parents as possible and ensures that parents are not inconvenienced by long wait times; it also lessens the impact on teachers' other responsibilities and their own out-of-school lives.

For parents from cultures that emphasize personal relationships, such closely timed meetings with minimal small talk and personal interaction may make them feel that the teachers are impersonal and disinterested because there is a (perceived) lack of caring about the person and the family (Trumbull et al., 2007). Such negative perceptions can create a sense of familial disconnect with the school and teachers, which can lead to low satisfaction with school, a lack of academic success, and poor behavior among students (Hill & Torres, 2010; Woolley, Kol, & Browne, 2008).

For many students entering U.S. universities, time management can be an issue when they come from cultures with more flexible attitudes toward time. For one, they may regard deadlines for homework assignments and other coursework as negotiable (Prowse & Goddard, 2010; Shapiro, Farrelly, & Tomaš, 2014). Another reason for time management issues is that in many educational systems globally, including most in the Middle East and Asia, the grade for an entire course is based on students' performance on a final exam (Ahmed & Myhill, 2016). Students coming from such an educational system face challenges in understanding the goals, tasks, and due dates of course assignments typical in the U.S., making successful time management, at least initially, demanding.

Language, Cultural Concepts, and Culture

Many cultural concepts such as time, family, love, anger, and so on occur across cultures. What varies is the understanding of how each of these cultural concepts is interpreted across cultures, such as in the discussion of time. Friendship is another example of a construct that appears to be universal; however, the conceptualization of what being a "friend" means in terms of who, when, and with what rights and responsibilities varies across cultures. Let's look at friendship in Germany. In German culture, the word "friend" (*Freund* / *Freundin*) is used only to indicate those to whom one has a strong personal connection, while "acquaintance" (*Bekannte* / *Bekanntin*) indicates everyone else. In Germany, it is much harder to make friends (*Freunde*), but when someone does make friends, these friends are truly friends in the sense that they will be there for that person, through thick and thin and over the long haul. In the U.S., people tend to make friends quickly and have various, and often temporal, friendships, which they tend to compartmentalize into "work friends," "school friends," "hockey friends," "mom's club friends," "Facebook friends," and so on (Gareis, 2000, 2012).

Although it has been suggested that the concept of friendship today represents something different from what it did before the advent of social media, counterarguments suggest that the concept of superficial friendships and true friendships has remained the same, but that the size of the superficial circle of friendship has grown (Amachai-Hamburger, Kingsbury, & Schneider, 2013). (Discussions on this topic can be located by searching the internet using the terms "friend" and "Facebook.") Research indicates that American students are more likely to have a larger superficial circle of "friendship" networks than, for instance, Chinese or Korean students. Researchers suggest that this is due to the American tendency to have more but fewer close friendships, whereas Asian cultures focus more on fewer but deeper friendships (Jackson & Wang, 2013; Kim, Sohn, & Choi, 2011).

Languages also have words that cannot necessarily be translated because the concepts they encompass are culturally derived. In Chinese, for example, there is the concept of *guangxi*, which is translated as "relationship or network among people often for the purpose of doing business." However, embedded within *guangxi* is also mutual trust and the development of strong personal ties, a balance of debts and obligations well beyond financial, and exchange of favors that may be very subtle, particularly to outsiders. *Guangxi* is therefore based on the preference of the Chinese to work within, and to favor members of, the in-group, whether this is their extended family, an organization or club they are members of, or their co-workers.

As these examples from German and Chinese illustrate, language is also a mirror of the speakers' culture. How is language a mirror of culture? We can think of language as a mirror when we consider how a given language reflects values, beliefs, norms, and worldviews central to its speakers (Deutscher, 2010). For example, the Korean culture is very hierarchical, which is reflected in the Korean language. Korean has a complicated system of *honorifics*, or special words that indicate respect, that speakers use in addressing each other. Speakers must base their choice of honorific on factors such as age and status, forcing Korean speakers to be cognizant of status, age, and hierarchy from the moment they learn to speak. If the person being addressed is older, even only slightly, the speaker must use a different honorific than if addressing someone younger (Yoon, 2005). To take another example, in Japanese even the most basic factual utterances convey information about status and relationship through verb choices and sentence elements in ways that do not exist in English (Matsumoto, 1989). These examples illustrate how the Korean and Japanese languages mirror their cultural norms of respect and social organization.

English does not have these types of constructions. It also does not, unlike many European languages such as Spanish, distinguish between a formal *you* used with people who are of higher status, older, or a stranger, and an informal *you* used with peers, friends, and family members. While it has been suggested that not having such grammatical features makes English a more egalitarian language (Crystal, 2012), English does use other means to indicate, for instance, respect—by sentence structure and word choices. These are not necessarily obvious to or immediately mastered by language learners, and students need to learn appropriate ways to engage with native speakers in different social contexts. For example, calling out to one's teacher in the classroom "Come help me" is unlikely to elicit the same response as "Could you help me, please?" (See Myth 5.)

We can see another example of language as a mirror of culture in English pronoun usage. In formal writing, the masculine pronouns *he, his,* and *him* have traditionally been considered the correct pronouns to use with indefinite pronouns such as *everyone, someone,* and *anybody*: "<u>Everyone</u> must bring <u>his</u> book to class." Yet, for centuries in spoken and informal written English, *they, them,* and *their* have been the preferred forms with these indefinite pronouns, as in: "<u>Everybody</u> must bring <u>their</u> book to class." The rationale behind the requirement for singular pronouns was that since indefinite pronouns were singular (*anyone, somebody*), the pronouns also had to be singular. Moreover, these default pronouns had to be masculine, which was related to the historical dominance of men over women and the exclusion of women from most of public life, whether from being property or business owners or from holding white-collar jobs, government positions, or other positions.

Recently, however, the use of plural pronouns *they, them,* and *their* with indefinite pronouns has increasingly become standard. This is a reflection of the trend in the English-speaking world for women to have active roles in public life as well as part of the push to be more inclusive of women and to be more gender neutral when possible. Many newspapers, such as the *Washington Post,* and most U.S. style guides now accept the use of *they, them,* and *their* after indefinite pronouns. But, because this change in formal usage is still controversial, language learners, as well as native speaker writers, may find themselves penalized in school and on standardized tests for using the impersonal plural pronouns rather than the singular forms with indefinite pronouns. This controversy shows how language mirrors the heterogeneity of culture. Teachers need to be aware of the controversy in order to help language learners distinguish between contexts where they can use the now more widely accepted plural pronouns and contexts where they must adhere to more traditional usage rules that may not reflect cultural (social) realities.

The Sapir-Whorf hypothesis (Whorf, 1956) offers another way to consider the interplay of language and culture. It posits that language and culture are intimately connected in that language determines how its speakers view and interpret the world. While a great deal of controversy has surrounded the Sapir-Whorf hypothesis since it was originally proposed, studies have indicated that because speakers' language obliges them to convey messages in specific ways, they will develop ways of thinking that differ from speakers of other languages. For example, English has only one definite article, *the*. No matter what the noun following is, *the* never changes because in English it is gender-neutral. Some languages, in contrast, vary the definite articles depending on the gender of a noun. In French and Spanish, all nouns, whether animate or inanimate, are assigned either masculine or feminine gender and take a different definite article accordingly. What research has demonstrated is how ingrained these gender categories are and how they shape native speakers' perceptions. When, for instance, French and Spanish speakers were given cartoons with various objects and asked to assign human voices to these objects, they almost always gave it the voice associated with the gender that noun has in their language. In French, fork is feminine (*la fourchette*); in Spanish, it is masculine (*el tenedor*). The French speakers preferred to give the fork a women's voice, while the Spanish speakers preferred a male voice (Deutscher, 2010).

When examining any given culture, we need to be aware of the tendency to assume that members of another culture are all the same, even when we become cognizant of the diversity within our own culture. Sub-group differences within a cultural can be as great or greater than differences across cultures (Kramsch, 1998a; le Roux, 2002). Within any culture, gender, socio-economic, regional, ethnic, linguistic and other differences exist. Northern Italy is different from southern Italy; northern China is different from southern China; the major northeastern cities in the U.S. are different from small towns in the South. Regardless of these variations, people are still products of their national cultures.

Having said this, we do want to avoid a perspective where "Mexicans do X," "Chinese do Y," or "Canadians do Z." Human behavior and cognition are complex and culture should not be reduced to a "heroes and holidays" view of culture (Nykiel-Herber, 2010) where the focus of lessons is solely or primarily on the stereotypical elements of culture such as foods, customs, dress, architecture, national or ethnic celebrations and festivals, and so on.

In addition, when we interpret people's behaviors as solely or primarily culture-driven, we run the risk of essentializing, stereotyping, and undervaluing the roles of identity, personality, and personal choices (Holliday, 2011). Atkinson (1999) and Atkinson & Sohn (2013) suggest that in exploring individuals and culture, we must consider the *cultural nature of the individual* and the *individual nature of culture*. The cultural nature of the individual refers to the sociocultural influences that contribute to each person's identity; the individual nature of culture refers to the elements of culture that individuals actively (although usually subconsciously) interpret, integrate, and construct through their experiences.

The Master's TESOL courses I have taught have had many Asian and Asian-American students in them. A common concern they raise in discussions on stereotypes is the stereotype of the "model minority": Asian students or students of Asian backgrounds work hard, excel in school, and are very good in math (Choi & Lahey, 2006). The students in my classes point out again and again that they have chosen to pursue a degree in teaching language, rather than the stereotypical Asian choice of computer science, engineering, or science, because they like languages and teaching and, very often, do not like or are not good in math. These students frequently feel the need to defend their choice when they encounter questions such as, "Why would you want to teach when you could earn a lot more money in (computer science)?"

Heping, a graduate student from China, shared a story from her student teaching experience in a U.S. high school: She was asked by her cooperating teacher and the assistant principal to tutor two students struggling with math, although she herself was getting her certification in ESL, was supposed to be student teaching in an ESL class, and was not good at math. Yet, based solely on her ethnicity, her American cooperating teacher and the assistant principal assumed she excelled in math.

As noted, the model Asian is a good stereotype—except that even "positive" stereotypes aren't always true and when something isn't true, people make wrong assumptions. While on the surface stereotypes such as these seem benign, they can lead to feelings of stress and anxiety when people don't fit the expected stereotypes, no matter how positive (Trytten, Lowe, & Walden, 2012).

Although our "business" is language, language teachers cannot and should not separate language teaching from culture when we consider that culture in large part is transmitted by and through language (Damen, 1987). By including culture in the language classroom, we need to move beyond units focusing on the visible elements of culture—heroes, holidays, and ethnic celebrations (Ngo, 2010) or the "dos and taboos" approaches. Instead, we want to explore culture to develop a deeper understanding of all that it entails and what it can and cannot influence. The goal is to evaluate rather than react emotionally when finding oneself in situations involving or having the potential to result in cultural misunderstandings. It is this type of *cross-cultural* learning that we want to infuse into our language teaching and learning.

What We Can Do . . .

1. Maintain a journal or blog.

Journals and blogs are excellent ways for pre-service and in-service teachers, as well as advanced language learners, to explore and document the development of their personal cross-cultural awareness. These journals or blogs should be maintained over a period of time to maximize deep reflection and to observe critically how one's understanding of cultural concepts changes. If *Culture Myths* is being used in a course, for example, each myth could be the basis of a weekly entry. Journal and blog entries could also be used to introduce or follow up on learning activities presented in the What We Can Do sections of each of the next six myths.

2. Evaluate what cultural knowledge students need to be successful in their setting.

Move away from focusing on visible aspects of culture such as holidays, dress, and food in your lessons. Instead, consider carefully what invisible elements of culture students should become aware of that will benefit them in adjusting to and participating more effectively in their new cultural environment. For instance, if your students are going to study at a U.S. university, what are the expectations for learning and how might they differ from those in their cultures? Use ongoing journals and blogs as suggested in #1 to help continuously evaluate students' cultural knowledge and needs.

3. Make use of resources on the internet.

After careful vetting on the part of the teacher, students can, for instance, watch and respond to short videos in which people experience or describe their encounters with cultural differences or misunderstandings. One video for introducing the topic of cultural differences that is a student favorite is a humorous HSBC ad in which a British businessman is at a dinner hosted by his Chinese colleagues. This is easily found on YouTube by searching "HSBC Eels Ad." In this clip, a British man is invited to dinner at a Chinese restaurant by his Chinese colleagues and host. He is served a bowl of cooked eel and, although shocked by this food item, methodically finishes his serving. His Chinese colleagues are stunned; the boss quickly orders the Brit another bowl, this time with even more eel, and so on it goes for a few more rounds, with the eel portions getting increasingly larger and the Chinese becoming increasingly frustrated. The humor here comes from a culture clash: In Britain, like in the U.S., good manners dictate that you finish everything to show your appreciation. In Chinese culture, on the other hand, cleaning your plate indicates that your host didn't provide you with enough to eat.

Another video that sparks conversation features intercultural couples talking about miscommunications in their relationships. This video can be located by searching "intercultural couples on miscommunication."

A good movie clip for discussion is the dinner scene in *Mr. Baseball*. In this scene, an American baseball player (Tom Selleck) living in Japan goes to a Japanese home for dinner. Searching "cross-cultural etiquette" and "Mr. Baseball" should locate the clip.

4. Structure discussions on specific topics.

Ask students to discuss questions on a specific topic. Questions and structured discussions can be tailored to meet the different needs of those in undergraduate or MA TESOL courses on culture, those in ESL classes, or those in content courses such as social studies.

Here are some sample questions on the topic of stereotypes:

- Have you ever been stereotyped? Or have you ever encountered stereotyping?
- What were your reactions? What were those of others?
- What were the sources of the stereotype?
- What stereotypes have you had about people from other cultures/subcultures that have changed? How did they change? Why?
- How are different cultures stereotyped in the media?

Alternatively, assign different students to be responsible for leading the discussion on select questions on different weeks and on different topics that have come up either in your class or in their lives.

5. Incorporate a variety of culture learning activities into all classes.

Learning activities can be structured differently depending on language proficiency, language focus, and curriculum content.

Sample Activity: Concepts and Cultural Values
1. Choose a pair of familiar and associated words such as *teacher* and *student* or *mother* and *child*.
2. Ask students to define the pair of words you have selected. Do the same but do not let the students see your work yet.
3. Make 2 columns, one for each pair you have selected.
4. Under each term, ask students to list what they see as the important characteristics or attributes of each.
5. Working in pairs or small groups, students compare and contrast their definitions and column lists with each other and with yours, which you should now share with them.
6. As a full class, discuss what underlying cultural values might be represented in definitions and lists.

This activity sample can be modified in different ways. If the content focus is social studies, for instance, you may choose words such as *democracy* and *dictatorship; grasslands* and *jungle;* or *urban, suburban,* and *rural.* This activity can become the basis for a writing assignment in a writing skills class or for a debate in an oral skills class. For related culture learning activities, see DeCapua & Wintergerst (2016): pages 44–47, "Values"; pages 97–99, "The Elephant in the Room"; and pages 142–143, "Semantic Associations."

6. Prepare mini-scenarios (critical incidents).

Mini-scenarios, also referred to as critical incidents, offer opportunities to explore cultural values and areas of misunderstandings and misinterpretations. There is not necessarily one right answer. Instead, they illustrate how multiple perspectives of the same situation derive from divergent, culturally influenced beliefs, norms, and worldviews (DeCapua & Wintergerst, 2016).

These mini-scenarios can be developed to meet the needs of different audiences, such as pre-service and in-service teachers or advanced language learners. The mini-scenarios can be used in a variety of contexts, whether in the K–12 classroom, university setting, or professional development workshops, or as food-for-thought for journal or blog entries.

The format, as illustrated, can vary. For example, you may supply the possible choices (see Sample Mini-Scenarios 1 and 3) or leave an open response for students to write their own choice (see Sample Mini-Scenario 2). In these samples, students examine each option in light of differing cultural attitudes and beliefs regarding time. They also consider how context, type of activity, status, and intimacy factors may influence choices. (Note: Care must be taken to avoid overgeneralization and stereotyping when using mini-scenarios.)

SAMPLE MINI-SCENARIO 1

You're meeting some classmates for a cup of coffee. You've agreed on 3:30 PM. It's now after 4 PM and everyone is just beginning to arrive. You've been waiting more than 30 minutes.

You are thinking:

A. Relax. 3:30 was just an approximate time.

B. How rude to keep me waiting for so long.

C. Everyone ultimately did show up, so why be annoyed?

D. When people make commitments, they should honor them.

SAMPLE MINI-SCENARIO 2

A student emails her professor to ask if she can come in to talk with her about some questions she has. The professor responds yes and they agree on Wednesday at 2:00 PM in the professor's office. The day and time come, the professor is in the office, and it is now 2:10; the student hasn't arrived. She arrives at 2:20.

In your opinion:

    A. The student should have called, emailed, or texted that she was running late.

    B. Since it was only 20 minutes, there wasn't a need for her to do anything.

    C. She wasn't very late, so an apology when she did get there would have been enough.

    D. Or, provide your own answer:

SAMPLE MINI-SCENARIO 3

Students are having trouble completing their assignments on time. Possible reasons for this may be:

    A. The students have difficulties understanding the language and content.

    B. The students come from polychronic or event-time cultures and have time management issues.

    C. The students are having trouble finding time to complete assignments because they have to work or take care of siblings.

    D. Students don't have anyone at home who could help them.

    E. Homework means something different in different cultures.

    F. The students may have different reasons why this is happening so teachers need to talk to each student individually.

    G. Maintaining family and social relationships is more important than completing assignments on time.

7. Start class on time but make provisions for latecomers.

Consider how you can begin class so that you do start on time, but so that latecomers will not disrupt or miss important work. This is not to say that you accept lateness, but as you work with these students on being more punctual, think about what you might do so that students who are on time will benefit and latecomers will be minimally disruptive. For example:

- Begin with a ten- to fifteen-minute activity that is engaging but meaningful to encourage students not to miss it. One popular activity is online polling using tools like Kahout.it or polleverywhere.com. Questions can be related to previous topics, the upcoming lesson, current events, or anything teachers choose.
- Avoid starting with procedural information that all students need to have.
- Before class begins, post or write a simple outline of the day's lesson. As you finish each part, check or cross it off. Doing this is common in elementary classes, but it is less so in upper grade levels and almost non-existent at the university level. Yet when lateness is a problem, visually providing these types of outlines helps students at any age understand the structure and objectives for the day, see clearly what they miss when they are late, and helps to promote punctuality.

8. Provide opportunities for students to analyze cultural information.

Using multicultural literature, for instance, helps students learn about, appreciate, and respect differences across culture. There is a wealth of such literature at different levels of English language proficiency and for different age groups. Good lists can be found on amazon.com, goodreads.com, and other websites by searching "multicultural books." Most sites offer previews, ratings, and reviews to help in selecting appropriate ones. Some commonly referenced ones are:

Alexie, S. (2012). *The Absolutely True Diary of a Part-time Indian.* Little, Brown Books.

Chua, A. (2011). *Battle Hymn of the Tiger Mom.* Penguin.

Cisneros, S. (1991). *The House on Mango Street.* Vintage.

da Costa, D. (2008). *Snow in Jerusalem.* Albert Whitman Prairie Books.

Diaz, J. (2007). *The Brief Wondrous Life of Oscar Wao.* Riverhead Books.

Hosseini, K. (2008). *A Thousand Splendid Suns.* Penguin.

Mobin-Uddin, A. (2005). *My Name is Bilal.* Boyds Mill Press.

Sanna, F. (2016). *The Journey.* Flying Eye Books.

Yang, G. L. (2008). *American Born Chinese.* Macmillan.

2

The goal of education is to develop each individual's potential.

In the Real World . . .

Some readers may be familiar with the U.S. Army recruiting slogan that was used for many years, *Be all you can be.* The inference is that joining the military, specifically the Army, will give individuals the opportunity to become that which they desire. Enlisting—joining by choice—puts them in control of their own destinies. The slogan is a reflection of the emphasis on individual choice and individual agency that is often considered a core value of mainstream U.S. culture and one that seemingly begins when children are infants by telling mothers that their babies should sleep in their own cradles or cribs. This practice, from the point of view of more interdependent cultures where mothers sleep with their infants, is often regarded as incomprehensible and even cruel (LeVine & LeVine, 2016).

The U.S. educational system, too, is centered on and promotes the individual—individual achievement, individual potential, individual needs, and individual development—along with an emphasis on personal choice, the achievement of personal goals, and the pursuit of reaching one's full potential (Hill & Torres, 2010). Many times I've had lively discussions with students and workshop participants about their notions of personal choice, free will, interdependence, independence, decision-making, and familial obligations. As a starting point, I often use these two items:

> Two roads diverged in a wood, and I—
>
> I took the one less traveled by,
>
> And that has made all the difference.

and

> Choose the path your ancestors have trod.

The first is an excerpt from a famous poem by the U.S. poet Robert Frost, *The Road Not Taken*. This excerpt (as well as the entire poem) emphasizes independence and the importance of making your own choices, both of which are highly valued in U.S. culture. Burger King, the popular hamburger fast food restaurant chain, provides another example of this. In 2014, the chain changed its slogan of the previous forty years from "Have It Your Way" to "Be Your Way." The company's rationale for the change clearly underscores the importance of the individual, just as the original slogan did by saying that people:

> . . . can and should live how they want anytime. It's ok to not be perfect ... . Self expression is most important and it's our differences that make us individuals instead of robots. ("Burger King Changes Slogan," 2014, para. 3)

The second item I use is a Cambodian proverb illustrating a very different viewpoint. What this proverb promotes is the importance of following in the footsteps of those who have preceded us and from whose experiences we can best learn. A new path or road is not necessary because the past will teach us the preferred or better way. My student Arshdeep for whom the Cambodian proverb deeply resonated, observed that the Indian extended family of people related by blood or marriage is everything, whether they are living in India or scattered around the world:

> Talking or thinking about "my decision" or "my life" is not part of the Indian mindset. It is the family who defines who you are and what choices you make. Your extended family shapes and passes on culturally prescribed values and norms and family is who you depend on for comfort, security, and well-being. It is also why arranged marriages are so important because a person doesn't marry just another person; a marriage conjoins two large, extended families with new extended relationships and obligations. Even when an Indian couple has children, each child's name is chosen with the help of the family because naming is a family endeavor, not just something the parents do.

Another story that illustrates contrasting perspectives on encouraging difference versus promoting cohesiveness is recounted by Brooks Peterson (2004, p. 3) as originally told to him by a U.S. expatriate in Japan. An American father visited his young daughter in her Japanese school and observed how, when presented with coloring books, the children would together all agree on which section of a picture to color first, agree on which color to use for that section, and then proceed to complete the same section with the same color. In the U.S., however, each child would individually choose a section, a color, and then color on his or her own. In the Japanese case, almost identically colored pictures exemplify the importance Japanese place on conformity. In the U.S., different results among a group of children exhibit the importance of individual expression.

A final story looks at the issue of choosing to be independent or alone. Lindsey, an outgoing, friendly U.S. graduate student, shared her story about living in Spain:

> Although I enjoy socializing, going out, and being with friends, I've also always loved alone time to read. At one time in my life I was teaching English in Spain and living in an apartment I shared with several Spanish friends. It was difficult for them to understand why I would decline an invitation to go out with them and other friends for a walk, meet up with others for a coffee, or do anything social. When sometimes I'd say that this time around I'd pass, stay home, and read a book, these friends become concerned that I was depressed, alienated, or whatever; they couldn't conceive that I needed time alone. For them, wanting to be alone and wanting only to read when I wasn't even a student indicated that something was wrong. As concerned friends, they felt the need to "help" me, when I really just wanted alone time. From their Spanish point of view, being with friends (and family) is central, and my declining to join them indicated I was in a bad place mentally. They knew me enough to know that I wasn't being rude, something these Spanish friends might have thought had they not known me as well as they did. What they had trouble grasping from their point of view was this desire to be alone. "Why would you want to be alone when we're all going to be together on this beautiful evening?" Or "You don't want to stay alone inside when it's so dreary out." It wasn't that they objected to my wanting to be alone, but what they couldn't fathom is how I would choose to be alone—to read—over being with friends.

What do these stories and these excerpts all have in common? All the stories and excerpts here reflect different cultural ways of looking at the world, specifically the concepts of *collectivism* and *individualism.* Do you decide to be all that you want to be for yourself (individualism) or do you decide based on what's best for everyone you consider important (collectivism)?

What the Research Says . . .

Collectivism and *individualism* are terms that describe how people in different cultures identify themselves with respect to others. In collectivistic cultures, people view themselves in terms of their relationships to others within what they perceive as their group. The perspective is that people survive, mature, and prosper within a network of complex social relationships; the group or "collective" is the center point of one's identity (Li, 2012).

The collective group may be the family, an extended kinship network, the clan, or another larger cultural or ethnic group. In West Indian cultures, such as Haitian and Jamaican, the group is the extended family, which includes aunts, uncles, and cousins of varying degrees of relationship, and non-blood members such as godparents (Ponzetti & James, 2003). In Mexico and other Latin American cultures, *compadragzo*, or familial support systems based on baptism and other rituals, are common (Gill-Hopple & Brage-Hudson, 2012). Large extended family systems are also the norm in the vast majority of the collectivistic sub-Saharan African cultures (Aryee, 2005).

In collectivistic cultures, people view the good of their group as more important than their own personal wants, desires, goals, and needs. Their priority is how their personal choices and achievements will benefit their group as a whole. Members of extended families provide financial and childrearing support to relatives beyond the nuclear family; older siblings routinely provide this same type of support for younger siblings. Siblings or other relatives will help each other, even if it means not purchasing something or postponing or interrupting their own studies. The collective good, in this case the family, is more important than that of a single individual. Luster et al. (2009) found that the issue of remittances was one area of conflict between Sudanese unaccompanied minors who were members of a collectivist culture and their U.S. foster parents (from an individualistic culture). The foster parents questioned the obligation the Sudanese youth felt to send as much money as they could back to others still in Africa. As one youth asserted,

> And I say these are my relatives, and she was like no, no, you don't have to send the money. That was a part of my money and I say that, you know, we share. We don't have money; they don't have money. If we have money, we need to share it together. (p. 391)

In collectivistic cultures, there is a greater awareness of and respect for hierarchy, and people are accorded status and respect depending on their age and societal role. Each person has social responsibilities and a role to fulfill as a member of the group (Zhang & Oetzel, 2006). What do I need to do to ensure the well-being and success of my group? That is the central question. Moreover, in collectivistic cultures like Spain or China, being alone is not generally regarded in a positive light. People prefer to be with other members of their group and are more inclined to feel isolated and lonely when not with the group than are members of individualistic cultures (Fokkema, de Jong, & Dykstra, 2012).

In individualistic cultures, people primarily identify themselves in terms of who they are as individuals. They see themselves as independent beings separate from others. This is not to say that people don't care about each other and that they don't have close relationships. The difference is in priorities. In individualistic cultures, people place more emphasis on personal self-interest and individual autonomy—for example, what are "my" desires, wishes, goals, and aspirations? These cultures tend to focus more on what each person can achieve and is capable of achieving for personal reasons and interests. Parents in individualistic cultures often promote their children's independence and self-reliance over strict authority and obedience, even at the earliest age (Tamis-LeMonda et al., 2007). In these cultures, people make an effort to "stand out from the crowd," and praise and reward for individual accomplishments are the norm. In the U.S., for instance, both women and men believe that being able to decide for themselves what they want to do for a living and having economic and social independence is fundamental (Badger, Nelson, & McNamara, 2006).

An easy way to conceptualize the difference between members of collectivistic cultures and individualistic cultures is by the two circles in Figure 2.1.

In the illustration on the left, the small circle within the large circle illustrates how individual identity is based on or derived from a person's group. The illustration on the right shows how individual identity, while related to a person's group, is still seen as separate from others.

Which cultures are more collectivistic and which ones more individualistic? In discussing collectivism and individualism, we want to keep in mind that we need to think of collectivism and individualism as existing along a continuum rather than as being two sides of a dichotomy. Some cultures will exhibit more values of collectivism and others more values of individualism. Highly

Figure 2.1. Collectivism and Individualism Circles

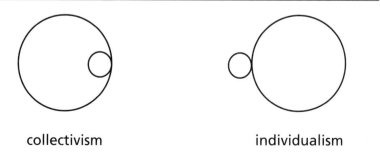

collectivism   individualism

collectivistic cultures, such as the Hmong and Guatemalan, would be at one end of the continuum, and highly individualistic ones, such as the U.S. and Canada, would be at the other end (Hofstede, Hofstede, & Minkov, 2010). Greece is less collectivistic than China, but more so than Germany (Triandis, 1995). Asian, Arab, most Latin American, and traditional African cultures are more likely to be collectivist than Northern European and Anglo-European cultures, such as Norway, the Netherlands, the U.S., and Canada (Northouse, 2007; Triandis, 1995).

While all collectivistic-oriented cultures are identifiable by the importance they place on the group and relationships, not all collectivistic cultures share all the same values and practices, given their very different histories. Latin American Spanish-speaking cultures are collectivistic cultures noted for the value of *familismo* or familism. The family is viewed as central in the life of the individual and the family is the collective. There is a deep sense of family closeness and interdependence among family members. Individual family members frequently subsume their personal preferences and decisions to those best for their family (Falicov, 2006; Steidel & Contreras, 2003). Parents, particularly fathers, are authority figures, and obedience and respect are highly valued (Halgunseth, Ispa, & Rudy, 2006). In the U.S., this sense of *familismo* has contributed to higher numbers of Latinas/os attending colleges or universities close to home so that the students are able to maintain strong family ties and to use the family network for support and guidance (Ríos-Álguilar & Kiyama, 2012).

East Asian cultures are highly collectivistic cultures that have been strongly influenced by the writings of Confucius, a Chinese philosopher from the late sixth century BCE. His teachings and work became the foundations of Confucianism, which emphasizes a hierarchical society centered on the maintenance of a stable and harmonious society through discipline and conformity, valuing the group over the individual, respect for age and tradition, and filial piety, or respect for one's parents and elders (Lee, Turnbull, & Zan,

2009). Conformity, being one of many, and not drawing attention to oneself are valued. The Japanese, for instance, have the saying, "The nail that sticks up gets hammered down."

Cultures such as those in China, Korea, and Japan place a very high value on *face*, which refers to the need to maintain (outward) harmony, respect, and dignity in one's interactions with others (Gudykunst, Ting-Toomey, & Chua, 1988; see also Myth 3 for more discussion). It is based on the desire to foster and maintain group relationships and group harmony, even if this comes at the expense of the individual (Matsumoto, 1988; Yu, 2011). Explicit disagreement or overt conflict, for instance, is avoided in preference for strategies that maintain social harmony and minimize animosity between the disputants (Gelfand et al., 2001). Camilla Vásquez, an American professor in Florida who taught in Thailand, recounted how different she found customer service interactions when she was living there: "When you had a complaint, you made it as politely, nicely and gently as possible, and you never became overtly angry" (C. Vásquez, personal communication, Sept. 2016). From the collectivistic perspective, preserving harmony, not making anyone feel uncomfortable, and allowing everyone to maintain face is central. From the American individualistic perspective of "The customer is always right" and that person's satisfaction and happiness is the top priority, there is no need to consider a balance in relationships in the same way. Of course, politeness is valued in the U.S. and no one likes a rude customer. We need only think of the saying "You catch more flies with honey than with vinegar." Nevertheless, the emphasis in the U.S. is on *me* rather than on *us*, and there is really no equivalent notion of face.

Another illustration of collectivism and individualism is the difference between Thai and American restaurant behavior. In the U.S., people may order an appetizer to share, but for the most part Americans each then order a main dish for themselves. In Thailand, all dishes are shared, and generally the senior person will decide which dishes to order and places the order for everyone.

Camilla also described what happened when a major U.S. restaurant chain entered the Thai market while she was living there: This chain prided itself on its extensive salad bar and each customer, after sitting down, received a small bowl for a single trip. For Thais, for whom sharing all food at a restaurant was standard, it never occurred to them that this single bowl was only for one person. They would go up in groups and cleverly "enlarge" the bowl by lining it with cucumber slices and lettuce leaves so that each bowl could be filled to the brim and higher with one salad item. All the bowls were then placed on the table for everyone to share. Americans, in contrast, take it for granted that they fill their small bowl with whatever salad items appeal to each person individually.

Another interesting example of different cultural perspectives on collectivism and individualism is evident in the 1998 Disney movie *Mulan*, based on the Chinese folktale *Ballad of Mulan*. The story is essentially about how a young woman, Mulan, disguised as a man, takes her father's place in the army when he is conscripted by the Emperor's men. She later succeeds in leading the army to victory against the enemy. Although the storyline is the same in both the original Chinese version and the Disney version, how the story is told and the underlying motivations ascribed to the characters, especially Mulan, embody cultural differences in core values, including collectivism versus individualism (Yin, 2013). The Chinese version emphasizes Mulan's loyalty to family and the collective good. Mulan's service as a warrior in the Emperor's army is done out of her strong sense of filial piety and duty to her country. When she returns home to her village, she immediately steps back into the role of the dutiful daughter, marrying the man her parents have chosen for her. The Disney movie version, in contrast, emphasizes Mulan's search for independence and personal achievement. Mulan takes her father's place as a means of finding her way as she struggles to be true to herself, despite the restrictions of her society. Disney Mulan is a symbol of personal achievement while Chinese Mulan is a symbol of duty and obedience to family and society— that is, to the collective good.

Like the original Chinese Mulan legend, folktales are a means by which important cultural values are transmitted (Imada & Yussen, 2012). Even when the comparable folktale is found in different cultures, diverse cultural values are apparent (Price, 1997). "The Three Little Pigs" is a popular folktale found in similar versions in many cultures. In the U.S. version, the story is about three pigs who each build a house, one of straw, one of sticks, and one of bricks. Here, values intrinsic to individualism are highlighted. The first two pigs are lazy and build their houses hastily and from flimsy material. When the big bad wolf comes, he is easily able to blow down their houses and eat them. The third industrious pig builds his house out of durable material and is thereby able to defeat and kill the wolf. The individual effort and hard work of the third little pig pays off in that only he survives (and triumphs over) the advances of the big bad wolf and lives happily ever after, albeit alone. In the Italian version, featuring three goslings rather than three pigs, the first two also build insubstantial houses, which again the big bad wolf easily blows down. The third gosling, another industrious character who builds her house out of iron and stone, tricks the wolf and also manages to kill him. In this version, however, the emphasis is on collectivism and group effort. After killing the wolf, the third gosling cuts open the wolf's stomach and her two siblings jump out alive. The three then all live happily ever after together. The third gosling's hard work benefits the good of the collective—in this case her sisters, who learn the error of trying to go it alone—and they all achieve happiness by living as a unit.

Cultural values are also reinforced in school texts. A study of Japanese and U.S. textbooks (Imada, 2012) found that stories in the U.S. textbooks focused on themes related to individualism, such as personal achievement. The stories generally featured a role model "who is a strong, distinctive individual, capable of achieving what he or she really wants" (p. 586), reminiscent of Disney's Mulan and her search for self-fulfillment. The Japanese textbooks, on the other hand, had stories that promoted themes related to the

Japanese concept of collectivism, such as conformity and group harmony. These stories emphasized characters who were considerate, generous members of the group, like Chinese Mulan who acted out of duty, both in joining the Emperor's army and later when returning home and marrying the man chosen for her by her parents.

In addition to stories in texts, in U.S. schools, the norms of collectivism and individualism are mirrored in and fostered by the educational system through the curriculum, by classroom dynamics, and by learning objectives and expectations (Hill, 2009). Students are encouraged to think for themselves and be separate, autonomous learners as they work to achieve their personal goals (Joyce, Weil, & Calhoun, 2014; Tamis-LeMonda et al., 2008). Furthermore, the type of instruction and learning activities that most commonly occur in the classroom reinforce individualism. Boykin, Tyler, & Miller (2005) report in their study that individualism was the most commonly occurring cultural concept, as determined by the amount of time students spent on individual learning activities (for example, doing worksheets or similar tasks) and responding individually after being called on by the teacher during whole class instruction.

The centrality of individualism in U.S. schools, whether manifested in the type of stories in textbooks, the curriculum, classroom dynamics, or other, can conflict with collectivistic values of students and their families. Kusserow (2004) reports that among the Somali Bantu, Sudanese, Vietnamese, and Hmong families in her study, the "self promotion and developing of self confidence promoted by . . . [the pedagogy] were considered selfish or obnoxious" (p. 473). As members of collectivistic cultures, these families valued conformity to norms, humility, and deference to authority, the opposite of what the schools were promoting. Similarly, Latino families, given their strong sense of collectivism centered on interdependent family relationships and respect for authority and obedience, struggle with the independence, self-expression, and assertiveness fostered among children in U.S. schools (Durand, 2011; Falicov, 2006).

Nevertheless, despite general, overarching cultural values and beliefs, it is essential to remember that, regardless of one's culture, people are still individuals. Within any given culture, some members will exhibit stronger and others weaker adherence to majority cultural features. Differences for the most part are found in how strongly members exhibit major cultural characteristics of collectivism or individualism. When individuals differ, they do so primarily by the degree to which they adhere to the cultural norms (Oyserman & Lee, 2008).

What We Can Do . . .

1. Be prepared for the fact that other cultures may view participation of family members in school activities differently than Americans.

For example, U.S. educators should be aware of and accept whenever possible that when they have elementary or secondary students from collectivistic cultures in their classes, the parents may bring along younger siblings or other extended family members to parent-teacher conferences or school-related events. Likewise, educators will find that it is not unusual for an extended family member or even close family friends to join in on school functions, especially when a student's parent cannot. From the collectivistic point of view, what constitutes a family member is wider and more fluid than what is generally accepted or acknowledged in the U.S. By being aware of these eventualities, educators can prepare to accommodate and provide for situations in which there could be issues of space, possible distractions from younger family members, or, from the U.S. perspective, concerns about confidentiality.

2. Avoid singling out individual students in the classroom.

Students from collectivistic cultures are not used to being singled out. Offer praise for work well done privately or commend students by writing comments on their assignments. Think of other ways to have students participate rather than calling on them individually. If students are uncomfortable speaking up in class, promote group or partner activities (see Myth 6). Make use of class blogs or discussion boards to encourage all students to participate equally.

3. Examine commercials or ads from popular U.S. chains such as McDonald's, KFC, or Nike.

Intermediate- and advanced-proficiency students or graduate students in TESOL can compare how ads and commercials produced for these companies emphasize collectivism or individualism depending on the culture in which they are promoting their goods. For instance, McDonald's ads for Asian markets often focus on families eating together. This activity can help students understand the primacy of certain values in collectivism and individualism. Many commercials and ads from across the world can be found on the internet and YouTube.

4. Explore children's storybooks and folktales.

Stories and folktales can be used to illustrate examples of behaviors, actions, or other things that may promote cultural values such as individualism or collectivism. Depending on students' language proficiency, choose books that will allow them to appreciate and discuss diverse cultural values. For example, the popular children's book *My Parents Think I'm Sleeping* (2008) by Jack Prelutsky shows how the actions of the main character extol individual decision over filial obedience. *The Adventures of Little Peachling*, a popular Japanese folktale available on the internet, emphasizes how group work brings success. A version of this for language learners can be found in Arengo's *Classic Tales Level 1 Peach Boy* (2016). There are also collections of folktales from around the world for ESL students available both in print and digitally.

5. Prepare mini-scenarios (critical incidents).

Give students mini-scenarios or critical incidents to explore contrasting cultural values, beliefs, norms, and worldviews (see Myth 1).

---SAMPLE MINI-SCENARIO

Luis and Mariana are quiet in class, never raise their hands when the teacher asks a question, and do not ask their teacher any questions. They appear disinterested and disengaged and have trouble completing class worksheet activities. This week, the teacher has the class working on a project in small groups. Now Luis and Mariana are different people; they are highly engaged and are actively participating.

Be sure the discussion focuses on specific targeted cultural concepts(s), not personality or language issues, while also avoiding overgeneralization and stereotyping. A discussion here could focus on how in some cultures, like the U.S., students demonstrate engagement by individually raising their hands to respond to teacher questions and by completing worksheet activities on their own in class. In cultures like that of Luis and Mariana, students show respect for teachers by listening and not asking questions and by commonly supporting each other in their learning.

6. Engage students in debates.

Ask your intermediate or advanced learners or graduate students in TESOL to debate dilemmas, with half taking the perspective of a collectivistic culture and the other half the perspective of an individualistic culture.

Sample Debate Scenario

Kamal is a refugee in the U.S. He is living with his older brother, is in high school, and has a part-time job. He receives daily calls or texts from his home country from people asking for money:

> "Your uncle needs money to pay for surgery or he will not be able to walk."

> "Your cousin needs money or he will go to jail."

> "Your cousin needs money to marry. It will shame the family if we can't pay for the feast."

> "Our neighbor's daughter needs money to pay her school fees or she will have to leave school."

> "Your uncle is being targeted since the coup. He needs money to flee."

How should Kamal respond? What should he do?

For Further Discussion:

How might your position change if Kamal

❑ could not work because of his immigration status?

❑ was not a high school student but had a full-time job to help his family here in the U.S.?

❑ was a girl?

Explain your reason(s).

7. Use folktales.

Folktales are highly stylized fantastical stories that illustrate the beliefs and values important in that culture and teach lessons. Find two or three folktales from different cultures that relate to teaching and learning. Ask the students to analyze what beliefs and values are illustrated in each one. How might these beliefs and values reflect their own classroom behaviors?

Example: *Stone Soup,* told in many cultures and easily available on the internet, illustrates the importance of working collectively for the good of the whole:

> The story takes place during a time of great famine when people were hoarding what little food they had. A traveler passes through a village, claiming he has a magic stone that will feed everyone. He pulls out a cauldron, fills it with water, lights a fire underneath, and carefully adds the magic stone. The villagers watch him, and one-by-one, bring something to add to the magic soup: carrots, onions, a little beef, and so on. Finally, the soup is finished and the whole village shares in the meal.

Focusing on conversational skills in the classroom is overrated.

In the Real World . . .

A number of years ago I went to a family reunion in Germany organized by some members of my mother's generation so that the younger generations would also get to know each other. Here I encountered some distant German cousins I had never met before. After preliminary introductions all around, we were left on our own to get to know one another. I started by asking one of them, *"Wie geht's?"* (How's it going?) to which she replied (in German) "How's it going? Yes, fine, I suppose." As an awkward pause ensued, I began chatting about the weather: How nice it was that the incessant rain had finally let up; that at least the flowers liked the rain; that I was looking forward to going for a walk once things got a little drier, and so on and so forth. She, along with another German cousin who had joined us, nodded at appropriate junctures, but neither contributed much of anything. When I ran out of weather topics, the other cousin turned to me and asked, "Do you really think George W. Bush deserved to win [the 2000 election]? And why did so few people turn out to vote?" I was, quite frankly, taken aback. I had just met these two cousins and we knew nothing about each other, yet they wanted to discuss U.S. politics? And voter turnout? This was a topic I couldn't remember having ever discussed before in a social setting with people I didn't know well. At this point I began to feel more and more uncomfortable, despite being fluent in German. After I said a few general things on these topics, we all three moved on to chat with other family members. Later, I described the situation to one of my close German cousins who had spent a year in the U.S. He laughed and said that the "problem" with Americans was that we always wanted to engage in small talk. He then added, "Germans don't do small talk."

A few years later I was involved in planning and supervising several high school summer study abroad programs for college credit. As part of the initial planning process, I went to each country to work with the local representatives on curriculum and to conduct professional development workshops for the teachers. One of the program sites was in Lima, Peru. For various reasons I was on a tight schedule, with little room for "extras." As soon as I arrived at the school site and after saying my hellos, I quickly laid out the agenda for the next two days. I was met with an awkward silence. I knew better, but feeling so very time pressured, I had ignored the golden rule prevalent in many parts of the world: "Start with the social, lead up to the business." In other words, personal small talk is *good*. While my "Let's get down to work" behavior would not have been a problem in the U.S., it did not make an initial good impression with my Peruvian colleagues. As we became more comfortable with each other, we were able to joke about my initial gaffe, and later they informed me that for being a Type A, I wasn't "all that bad." I also learned to be comfortable with "small talk" that included topics I wasn't comfortable with except with close friends, such as how much I paid for something, physical features, and controversial political events.

What the Research Says . . .

The lesson we can draw from these anecdotes is that a conversation in another language is not just something conducted the same way but in a different language. Each language not only has its own vocabulary and grammar, but also has its own sociocultural norms governing communicative interactions. Conversation goes well beyond language in that you can be grammatically correct in all you say, but what you choose to say, and how and when you choose to say it, are not the same across cultures. Like with all elements of culture, however, we must be very careful not to overgeneralize when it comes to how we communicate. Because language and culture are intricately intertwined, speakers will employ shared (and largely implicit) critical, non-linguistic norms of speaking, which will differ across cultures. These include knowledge of nonverbal behaviors (Myth 4), what factors in a given conversational setting demand attention, and the role of variables such as age, gender, and status (see Myth 5). With any language, age, status, gender, and intimacy considerations affect the nature of conversation (Angouri, 2010; Kottholf & Spencer-Oatey, 2007). Yet there are observable differences in how conversations are conducted across cultures because speakers follow culturally shared communicative conventions and norms (House, 2012; Kramsch, 1998b). These include how much small talk there should be (if any), which topics are considered appropriate (or not) when in conversation with different types of people or in different situations, and how turn-taking happens in a conversation.

Small Talk

In the U.S., people generally start conversations with *small talk*, a technique to create a pleasant, safe exchange when meeting strangers or talking with acquaintances, usually about neutral topics such as weather or sports. We use small talk to test the social waters in many types of verbal interactions to determine whether we want to continue building a relationship, develop a deeper friendship, or for networking purposes. We use small talk to create a positive, friendly atmosphere before business meetings, job interviews or other high-stakes events, and in everyday social settings.

When we make small talk with people we don't know well, we stick to neutral topics. For the most part, the list of neutral topics appropriate for small talk in the U.S. is relatively short and includes weather, sports, entertainment (movies, TV shows, music), food (popular restaurants, cuisines), and travel.

Small talk may also include compliments such as, "That's a nice sweater you're wearing" or "Nice catch on that fly ball." The expected response is to graciously accept the compliment or downplay it, as in "I got it on sale" or "Thanks, I really got lucky" (Manes, 1983; Wolfson, 1981). However, the appropriate responses to small talk compliments—or the use of small talk in general, for that matter—are not the same across cultures. For example, in Chinese culture, recipients of small talk compliments are expected to demonstrate their humility, as in "No, no, it's a very old and ugly sweater" or "I was very stupid" (Chen & Yang, 2010; Yu, 2005).

Although the content of small talk may not be particularly important, engaging in small talk in U.S. and other English-speaking countries is seen as playing an important social role (Coupland, 2000, 2003; Holmes & Stubbe, 2015). The ability to engage in appropriate small talk is an essential prelude to continued social interaction, particularly in the workplace, where it can improve workplace dynamics (Louw, Derwing, & Abbott, 2010; Mirivel & Tracy, 2005). Engaging in successful small talk with a U.S. citizenship test examiner can even be a make-or-break factor in whether an applicant passes (J. Flaitz, personal communication, October 24, 2017).

Yet, other cultures, such as German culture, the same concept of small talk does not exist (House, 2006); in fact, when referring to small talk, Germans use the English phrase *Small Talk* (Germans capitalize nouns) because there is no equivalent concept in German. When interacting in situations where Americans would engage in small talk, Germans prefer more substantive topics such as politics or, in the case of a business meeting, prefer to get on task immediately (Köhler, Cramton, & Hinds, 2012). Although the phrase *small talk* has been adopted by Germans, it is still not a comfortable or familiar concept for many (Kilian, 2015).

Too Personal or Not?

What topics are considered appropriate in conversational interactions varies across cultures. In small talk, acceptable topics in one culture may be intrusive or off-putting in another. Peruvians, like most Latin American cultures, favor small talk topics related to family or the country, such as geography, history, and places of interest. In the U.S., topics such as one's political views, religion, or salary are generally off limits (Emily Post Institute, 2011; Gabor, 2011). Because these topics are regarded as personal information— or they could lead to revealing personal information—they are not necessarily shared with strangers or casual acquaintances. In instances when these topics are raised with strangers, it often creates an uncomfortable or negative atmosphere, rather than rapport-building small talk. Specifically, sharing one's political or religious views can be seen as incendiary or proselytizing; when people talk about how much money they have made or how much their children earn, it is seen as bragging or boasting. In contrast, in India, talking about earnings is an everyday topic (Lubin, 2013). Likewise, Chinese parents are known to tell other people what their children earn as well as all about their children's lives because doing so reflects positively on the family as the collective whole.

Other off-limit topics in the U.S. include negative comments on a person's weight or appearance. It is very rude to remark on how unhealthy a person looks or on how wrinkled one's face is, for instance. In other countries, such as India, these comments are not necessarily seen as rude but are simply factual comments that can indicate concern and caring. And in some countries, telling a woman that she looks fat is a compliment since plumpness signals prosperity. Guyana tour guides for Americans visiting their country had to be specifically instructed not to say things like "Ah, packing it on—good deal!" to overweight Americans (Weed, 2016). In the U.S., where the ideal of a beautiful woman has become associated with being model-thin, such a comment is anything but complimentary.

Topic appropriateness is not only a consideration in small talk. What kinds of questions are considered too personal or off limits when conversing with people who are not in one's circle of family and close friends is not always the same across cultures. Female ESL teachers in the U.S. frequently tell stories of "inappropriate" personal questions and comments they have received. Stephanie and Nancy, two middle-aged ESL teachers, described how they had been asked many times how old they were and how many children they had, by both their students and the families of their students. When they would say that they weren't married and didn't have children, they received responses ranging from, "Your father, he give you no money to marry" to "My brother looking for a wife, but you too old to have many children," to "I'm so sorry for you die alone."

Much of what is considered personal is related to a culturally based concept of what encompasses the private sphere versus the public sphere, which are related to individualism and collectivism (see Myth 2). Qin (2014) describes how uncomfortable an American student in China felt when she was asked by strangers how much her parents earned, if she was married, or if she wanted a Chinese boyfriend. For Americans, these are intrusive questions that are "nobody's business" because Americans view these as belonging to an individual's private sphere. For Chinese, such questions are simply a way of engaging in conversation because they are perceived as falling within the public sphere. Moreover, the concept of privacy as understood in the U.S. and other Western cultures is relatively recent in China (Mintner, 2016).

Asking very personal questions such as inquiring why a woman is unmarried or why a couple is childless is common in many cultures. My student Amira recounted how in Egypt, there are many personal questions that people ask and it is not unusual for a woman to be asked about her marital status. The speaker begins with a statement such as, "You look very beautiful for your age. Are you married?" If one replies that one is not married, the speaker will think nothing of responding with "Why NOT? You must be very demanding." An American colleague, female and single, who has worked extensively with educators from Middle Eastern and Latin cultures has had similar experiences and even had one person ask her, "What is wrong with you?"

The Choreography of Conversation

Small talk and topic appropriateness are only two aspects of conversational skills. Conversation can be viewed as a choreography of speech: There is a conversational "dance" where the moves depend on each person (subconsciously) following independent, yet inter-dependent, patterns. A smooth choreography depends on speakers sharing the same norms of conversational participation. Even highly proficient non-native speakers may encounter challenges and mis-understandings during conversations with native speakers (Moran, Abramson, & Moran, 2014), as do native speakers themselves (Renee et al., 2017). Regardless of language proficiency, speakers need to realize that there are cross-cultural differences in how con-versations are formed (Carbaugh, 2005). As in the story about small talk with my cousin, the response did not provide an *uptake,* or cue, for continuing the dialogue. Instead her response quickly ended the conversation and created an awkward pause.

Another way to choreograph conversations is the use of *backchannel cues* (Yngve, 1970). These are verbal (e.g., *uh-huh, mm-hm, yeah, okay* in English) and non-verbal cues (e.g., smil-ing, head nodding) produced by listeners to indicate that they are paying attention to the speaker. In instances where these verbal and non-verbal cues differ across cultures, a speaker may misinter-pret the other's intent (Li, 2006). Research indicates that Japanese speakers use backchannel cues more frequently and in different places within conversation than do American speakers (Maynard, 1997). In conversations between Americans and Japanese, the Americans may subconsciously wonder why the Japanese are nod-ding so often (high use of a backchannel cue) and whether this means they aren't really listening or understanding. The Japanese, on the other hand, may wonder why the Americans aren't nod-ding all that much (low use of a backchannel cue) and whether it means they aren't paying attention, or could it even subtly signal disagreement?

Other areas of difference are pause length and the amount of talk itself. In some cultures, relatively long pause lengths between speakers are considered appropriate, while in others, interruptions and overlaps are the norm (Stivers et al., 2009). Technically, an interruption takes the floor away from the speaker—that is, it does not allow the current speaker to continue his or her turn. Inherent in interruptions is the feeling of infringement of a speaker's rights. By not waiting for an appropriate pause length—whatever that may be understood to be—and wresting away the speaker's turn, the new speaker intrudes onto the current speaker's verbal territory (Hutchby, 2008; West & Zimmerman, 1983). An *overlap* is when one or more voices speak simultaneously without attempting to grab the floor away from the current speaker. Overlaps, even though they take place during another speaker's turn, function as supportive speech because they reiterate, rephrase, agree with, or request additional information from the current speaker without forcing that person to relinquish the floor. They are a means by which speakers express empathy, solidarity, concern, involvement, and camaraderie (DeCapua, Berkowitz, & Boxer, 2006; Tannen, 2005).

While there is agreement on the definition of interruptions and overlaps, there is not always consensus on what constitutes either one in communicative interactions. In the U.S., for example, there are noticeable regional differences. To outsiders, New Yorkers are often seen as brusque and rude because, in the New York City metropolitan area, pause times between speakers are shorter and speakers engage in more overlapping and interruptions than do speakers in other regions (DeCapua, Berkowitz, & Boxer, 2006; Tannen, 2005). But, it is all a matter of perspective. As Deborah Tannen (2005) found in her famous Thanksgiving dinner study of a group of friends from California and New York, the Californians felt the New Yorkers dominated the conversation while the New Yorkers felt the Californians didn't have all that much to say. Tannen's analysis of the video recording attributes much of this to differing interpretations of appropriate pause length and what constituted an interruption versus an overlap between Californians and New Yorkers.

I had a similar experience when I moved from the New York City area to Louisville, Kentucky. At the time, I had young children and was involved in various playgroups, mommy-and-me events, and similar programs. After several months, I was told by some of the mothers that I was rude and too often tried to take over conversations. As a linguist and someone familiar with Deborah Tannen's work, I came to the realization (and after getting over the hurt) that these southern mothers had a different conversational style. In becoming more of an observer and less of a participant, it became obvious to me that there were clearly longer pause lengths and fewer overlaps than what I was used to. It took effort, but eventually I learned to adapt my conversational style to theirs during the three years I lived there.

Across cultures we see even greater differences. In conversational exchanges, Japanese generally use longer pauses than do speakers in the U.S. The Japanese language has a term *ma*, which can be roughly translated as "space between things." *Ma* can be used for many kinds of spaces, including pauses in conversation, considered to be as important as verbal discourse (Di Mare, 1990). It's the case in many cultures that speakers take time to reflect after they have been asked a question; this indicates that one is taking the time to consider one's response carefully, whereas responding quickly, as Americans tend to do, is seen as an indication of a lack of thought (Bista, 2012).

Finns are known for enjoying long stretches of silence, even in the presence of others; there is even a well-known joke by Finns about this (variations of this joke can be found on the internet):

> Two Finns, Mikko and Otto, have been sitting in a bar for several hours drinking a bottle of vodka in silence. After ordering another bottle of vodka, Mikko turns to Otto and says, "Cheers" to which Otto replies exasperated, "Did you come here to drink or to talk?"

Americans, on the other hand, are typically uncomfortable with silence and will jump in to fill in gaps in conversation. In a discussion on the topic of silence in conversation, an American student, Connie, noted:

> When there's nobody saying anything and there's just silence, it's uncomfortable. Everyone feels awkward until someone says something, even if everyone is staring at their smartphones and it's just something like, "Look what just came up on my Instagram" or "Listen to this tweet from . . ." There's this need to break the silence, even when you have nothing in particular to say.

In the Classroom

In the classroom, feeling uncomfortable with (perceived) stretches of silence frequently translates into teachers not allowing sufficient wait time after asking a question, particularly in the case of language learners (Ingram & Elliott, 2014). Language learners generally require a longer wait time than native speakers as they work to organize and present their thoughts in their new language (Zarrinabadi, 2014). In addition, cultural factors regarding appropriate pause time, as we have seen, can also play a role. As teachers, it is essential to become attuned to how long a pause really is rather than how long it feels (King, 2013; Walsh & Sattes, 2016). A good suggestion is to look at a clock and make sure that you allow at least a full 60 seconds for a student to respond to your question before either jumping in or turning to another student.

At the same time, teachers need to be conscious that in some cultures speakers use very short pauses or no pause time, leading to more overlaps and interruptions than generally acceptable in English. Israeli Hebrew and Spanish speakers, for instance, demonstrate conversational engagement through frequent conversational interruptions (Ardila, 2004; Zupnick, 2000), and they may transfer this behavior into English. Because interruptions are not necessarily evaluated as negative conversational behavior in their cultures, these speakers may not realize that English speakers generally find interruptions disconcerting and annoying.

Gender also plays a role in interruptions and conversational dominance; men tend to interrupt women more than women interrupt men (Coates, 2014). Much of this is learned behavior, which appears to be formed at an early age and is reinforced by cultural norms that value male contributions over female ones (Julés, 2004). In the classroom, when women come from cultures where they traditionally play a subordinate role to men, they may find it challenging to actively participate in mixed-sex class discussions or keep the floor when they are speaking. Teachers will want to pay attention to classroom participation patterns and try to take measures to encourage equal participation among all students (see Myth 5, What We Can Do).

At the university level, some of the communication styles of international graduate students that teach undergraduates have led to cross-cultural miscommunications and misunderstandings in university classrooms (Li, Mazer, & Ju, 2011). These instructors, known as International Teaching Assistants (ITAs), often face challenges hindering effective communication and teaching. In addition to the readily apparent difficulties related to accents and comprehensibility, ITAs may also have divergent communication styles from those of U.S. students. Conflicting communication styles have led to negative perceptions of ITAs by U.S. students and have impacted student learning and satisfaction (Comadena, Hunt, & Simonds, 2007). As we have seen, for instance, U.S.-style small talk plays a crucial rapport-building role for positive interpersonal interactions. This includes interactions taking place between instructors and students, whether in the classroom or during office hours.

Knowing when and how to use small talk may appear unimportant to the casual observer, but its importance in fostering positive interactions between teacher and student may be a significant factor in the successful integration of ITAs in U.S. classrooms and their success in teaching undergraduates (Staples, Kang, & Wittner, 2014). In short, since conversational norms differ across cultures, we want to ensure that we, as teachers, and our students become attuned to areas that might cause cultural misunderstandings or communication breakdowns and lead to adverse evaluations and/ or stereotyping of non-native speakers.

What We Can Do . . .

1. Offer structured opportunities for conversational practice in the classroom.

Developing effective communication skills entails both language and cultural awareness. Providing language learners with different contexts and opportunities to practice their language skills and develop cultural awareness is important in any language class-room. Asking language learners to participate in plays, skits, and role-plays are fun options. By structuring these to meet student needs and goals, they also promote the development of targeted conversational skills. For example, if students are preparing to enter the workplace in an English-speaking environment, foster their small talk skills by designing skits or role-plays where they need to engage in small talk during a job interview, before a meet-ing, or when socializing with colleagues or co-workers.

Plays, skits, and role-plays can be differentiated for any level of proficiency and structured in various ways, ranging from semi-structured, teacher- (or textbook)-created dialogues to completely open-ended performances.

2. Encourage students to become good observers.

It is often very difficult to "see" cultural differences in conversational norms. An effective way to help learners become explicitly aware of such differences is by having students view clips from TV shows, movies, YouTube videos, and similar media. To help them tease out which aspects of the conversation(s) to pay particular attention to, teachers can prepare a short graphic organizer, similar to this one:

Sample
Title of movie from which clip was chosen: **Outsourced**
Setting (brief summary of scene) **Todd, an American, arrives at a guest house where he is effusively greeted by the owner, Aunti Ji. She serves him tea and snacks and begins grilling him.**
Participants (age, gender, relationship, etc.) **Todd, an American from Seattle, Washington** **Aunti Ji, an older Indian woman and the owner of the guest house where Todd is staying**
Topic(s) of the conversation **Personal questions to Todd such as, "What does your father do?" and "Are you married?" from Aunti Ji, a person he had never met before.**
How was the conversation maintained (or not maintained)? **Todd feels very uncomfortable and has trouble answering questions he feels are an invasion of his privacy. We see this in how Todd hesitates in responding to Aunti Ji and how he avoids looking at her.**

For additional suggestions, see DeCapua & Wintergerst (2016), pages 303–308, "Learning to Look."

3. Let students practice becoming conversation problem-solvers.

Provide students with mini-scenarios (critical incidents) that illustrate communication misunderstandings. Ask them to explore reasons why these misunderstandings may have occurred and suggest alternative ways of conducting the conversation. (See Myth 1, What We Can Do.)

SAMPLE MINI-SCENARIO 1

The school year has just started and you are hoping to make friends with some of your new classmates. You go over to introduce yourself to one of them: "Hi, my name is ____. I'm new. I want to be your friend. What a big nose you have!" The classmate looks surprised and irritated and then moves away without responding. You then go over to another classmate: "Hi, I'm ____ from ____. You have such nice wide hips, perfect for children."

A scenario such as this one provides opportunities for students to discuss and compare conversational scripts, social conventions, and topic appropriateness. Such a scenario can also be a starting point for students to create and practice appropriate English dialogues and role-plays.

SAMPLE MINI-SCENARIO 2

It is orientation day and after a formal presentation by school staff, parents are invited to meet with their children's teachers. Mrs. Kasongo, who speaks excellent English and has just moved to the U.S. with her family, is excited to be meeting her son's teacher. After Ms. Wilson finishes briefly reviewing the curriculum and her expectations, Mrs. Kasongo comes up, introduces herself, and thanks Ms. Wilson for becoming a teacher. Ms. Wilson smiles and nods her head. Mrs. Kasongo continues, "How much do you get paid? Is it enough reward for your so many responsibilities and dedication?" Ms. Wilson, after a pause, responds, "Yes, well, we all do our best" and turns to another parent.

Like in Sample 1, students can discuss topic appropriateness in Mrs. Kasongo's culture versus in Ms. Wilson's culture. For Mrs. Kasongo, asking someone about her salary appears to be a standard conversational topic, perhaps a form of—from her perspective—appropriate small talk. Ms. Wilson, on the other hand, is taken aback (c.f. "after a pause") by what she views is a personal, "none of your business" question and avoids giving an answer. She also forces an end to the conversation by turning to another parent.

SAMPLE MINI-SCENARIO 3

Jun-young is a doctoral candidate in chemistry. His doctoral advisor, Dr. Bustamante, has invited him and two of the other doctoral students out to dinner to welcome them at the beginning of the semester. Dr. Bustamante's wife, Dr. Tauber, a law professor, is with them at the restaurant. Jun-young is seated between Dr. Tauber and one of the other doctoral candidates. During the meal, Jun-young talks only about chemistry. Later, after the dinner, Dr. Tauber says in an annoyed tone to her husband, "Once again we had an international student who had nothing to say that wasn't related to chemistry, which of course left me out of the conversation."

With a mini-scenario such as this third one, students can first explore what Dr. Tauber's expectations about appropriate conversational behavior in a social setting might be. The discussion can then expand to considering different contexts and with varying constellations of participants—professional, social, collegial, a mix of professional and social, and so on. This type of mini-scenario also allows students to identify what communicative skills they feel the need to practice.

4. Listen to and analyze conversations.

Numerous websites offer examples of conversations at different English language proficiency levels. A search using a phrase such as "practice English conversations" will return many results. Some of these will be of higher quality than others, so teachers should carefully evaluate which one(s) they want to recommend to their students.

For advanced-proficiency learners, there are many YouTube videos geared to native speakers of American English that address developing strong conversation skills, such as avoiding having another speaker take away the floor or basic conversation start-ers. Such videos can be used to help students explore the different values underlying the suggestions, as tips for improving their own conversational skills, and as the basis for developing their own skits and role-plays for practice (see #1). These types of videos can be found by searching "stop interruptions" or "conversation start-ers." One helpful YouTube video that focuses on specific helpful small talk strategies to use in conversation and that is appropri-ate for high-intermediate language proficiency students and up can be located by searching "better conversations using the FORD method."

MYTH 4

Not looking at the teacher shows disrespect.

Janine from Atlanta, Georgia, told a story in class about a young Russian family who moved into her neighborhood. Several of her mother's friends criticized the Russian mother as being aloof and unfriendly because she never smiled and barely nodded her head in acknowledgment when they greeted her as she was walking her baby around the neighborhood. What these Americans didn't know is that Russians don't smile at strangers. The young Russian mother wasn't being rude to her new neighbors; she was following the non-verbal norms of behavior of her culture.

An American colleague who went on Fulbright to Sweden shared a similar situation but from the other side: "Although I knew that the norm for smiling at strangers was different, it was still disconcerting for me as a Midwesterner (in the U.S.) to stand in an elevator or walk by someone in the hallway apartment complex, even if I didn't know them, and not smile, or, if I forgot and did smile, to get a strange look."

Gina describes how during her student teaching while participating with her cooperating teacher in parent-teacher conferences,
she initially felt hurt and put off by the behavior of the immigrant
parents of the children because they never smiled. As an American,
Gina expected the parents to indicate friendliness by smiling; however, as she later learned from her cooperating teacher, in many
cultures, smiling as an indicator of friendliness is reserved for close
friends and family members.

Most people today are aware of the term *body language*, or the
more encompassing term *non-verbal communication*. Both refer to
how we communicate messages to others without using speech.
Facial expressions, eye gaze, body movements and gestures, personal space, posture, and orientation are all grouped under the
umbrella of non-verbal communication. Everyone everywhere
engages in some sort of non-verbal communication to convey
attitudes, intentions, and emotions. Even when we're not speaking, we're sending messages via our non-verbal behaviors. At this
junction, let me make clear that when we talk about non-verbal
communication, we are referring to *a shared code of behaviors among
members of culture*, not one person's idiosyncratic body language.

Certain aspects of body language are universal, specifically facial
expressions related to the six basic emotions: anger, disgust, fear,
sadness, happiness, and surprise. There is even a saying, "The eyes
are the window to the soul." The key to understanding the "window
to the soul," however, is very much culturally based. The six basic
emotions themselves are universal, but non-verbal communication
codes are not. If you don't know the code, you will not be able to
interpret correctly the meaning a speaker is trying to convey. Because
the types, meanings, and degree of intensity of non-verbal behaviors
differ across cultures, cultural stereotypes have resulted, such as the
"forcefully gesticulating Italian male" or the "inscrutable Asian."

When do we use non-verbal communication? One reason that
we use non-verbal behaviors is to replace verbal language. This
may be something as basic as nodding one's head up and down in

the U.S. to indicate yes or agreement. Or, it may arise from necessity, such as when we're in a situation overseas where we don't know or have little proficiency in the language of that country and we are trying to get a message across, although not always successfully. My high school Spanish teacher liked to tell the story of traveling in Morocco and trying to convey the idea of "chicken" in a restaurant by flapping her arms and bobbing her head. On one very memorable occasion this resulted in the restaurant owner bringing her a live chicken.

We also use non-verbal behaviors to reinforce or underscore what we're saying. With students from diverse cultures in our classrooms, interpreting non-verbal behavior can be challenging on both sides since understandings of the intended meaning may conflict. In English, when you want to indicate someone's height, we sometimes gesture with the palm of our hand facing down. One of my students, Alyssa, a middle school math teacher, related a story about this involving one of her Mexican immigrant students:

> We were doing ratios and proportional relationships. I had some of the kids at the front of the room, was saying something like, "and if you're this tall" and gestured with my hand, palm down "or this tall," and went on with looking at different problems on proportions, height, weight, and so on. Later in the week, I got a call from one of the mothers, who told me her son came home upset. It turns out that in Mexico, this gesture for height is only used for animals!

In my work with pre-service and in-service teachers, as well as with administrators, I often encounter comments along the lines of "Jeni never looks me in the eye when I'm asking her if she understands" or "When the parents or guardians come for a conference, no one will look at us when we're speaking." One time as I was signing in at a school to do a student teacher observation, I overheard a conversation between a Latina student and an administrator. The student had been sent to the office for being disrespectful and the teacher "had had enough." As it turned out, it all hinged on the student not making the conventional U.S. eye contact with her teacher. What we see here is a clash: Mainstream U.S. culture expects people to look each other in the eye during conversational exchanges to indicate attention and respect. Other cultures interpret looking at each other in the eye as disrespectful, or, in the case of a man looking at a woman or vice versa, as having a sexual connotation.

No interpretation of non-verbal communication is wrong or right; it is the context that is important. Just like one shoe does not fit all, so non-verbal communication is not all the same but rather culturally situated: Who is involved and what is the gender, social status, age, and cultural background of the speakers? The difficulty comes in needing to correctly "read" the non-verbal behaviors of someone from another culture.

Non-verbal behavior is complex, including more than just body movements. At one time I was tutoring a Japanese businessman. One day after our session, I started to confirm dates for the upcoming month. He opened his calendar, kept tapping through dates without ever making eye contact with me, and slowly, very slowly with long pauses, repeating, "So sorry . . . very busy . . . very busy . . . this month . . . very busy . . . very busy . . . this month." It took me some time to realize that he was indirectly signaling to me that he didn't want to be tutored (at least by me) anymore. At that point, I said to him that it had been a pleasure tutoring him and that he should contact me when he wasn't busy. His indirect style of ending our sessions through his (primarily) non-verbal behavior allowed both of us, from his perspective, to maintain face. He didn't have to actually say that he didn't want to work with me anymore, which would have implied that there was something wrong with me. He carefully avoided looking at me, while continually looking at his calendar as he painstakingly clicked through it. In addition, despite the fact that his English was quite good, he repeated only a few short phrases, rather than producing more complex utterances.

Teachers may find themselves in similar circumstances where parents or students from other cultures use non-verbal behaviors to send a message that is unclear because they don't share the same code. Judy, a high school ESL teacher, described how her Vietnamese and Bhutanese students who had not completed homework assignments would diligently search through their papers, essentially behaving like the Japanese businessman. When this first happened, Judy took their behavior to mean that they had misplaced their work. Later, after becoming more familiar with their cultures, Judy realized they were indirectly signaling her that they hadn't done the assignment rather than verbally saying so, thereby saving face. In short, non-verbal behaviors are an effective way of communicating information—if people share the same code.

What the Research Says . . .

Many basic functions of non-verbal communication are found across cultures, including but not necessarily limited to: expressing emotions; supporting, emphasizing, or even contradicting verbal messages; conveying information in a ritualized form; and substituting for verbal communications (Ekman & Friesen, 1969; Patterson, 1990).

How much of our communication consists of non-verbal messages? Most people believe it is less than half, but research indicates that more is communicated through body language than through verbal exchanges, as much as 93 percent. But what is this based on? In the late 1960s Albert Mehrabian and associates conducted two experiments on groups of participants, all native speakers of English (Mehrabian & Ferris, 1967; Mehrabian & Wiener,

1967). Although the experiments focused on the communication of emotions in a very limited context, this 93 percent formula has been widely cited and extrapolated to all forms of non-verbal communication, without regard for type, context, or culture (Lapakko, 1997). Another influential early researcher, Ray Birdwhistell (1952, 1970), who focused on a broader approach to non-verbal communications, suggested that approximately 65 percent of communication occurs non-verbally. While doubts also remain with regards to this percentage (Burgoon, Guerrero, & Floyd, 2010), it is clear that non-verbal behaviors communicate a great deal of information (Kim, 2001; Moreno-Cabrera, 2011). And, regardless of any percentages, we must realize that non-verbal communication cannot be understood outside of its cultural context (Jones & LeBaron, 2002; Matsumoto, 2006).

Researchers have roughly categorized cultures into two types. Cultures that favor personal closeness and encourage close contact between members are categorized as *high-contact* cultures. Members from such cultures stand closer together, touch more often and more openly, and use more body movements and with higher degrees of intensity than do members of the second category, low-contact cultures. Members from *low-contact* cultures prefer greater personal distance and less personal contact, and are more subdued in their use of body movements (Hall, 1966). This distinction between what is high and low contact is very broad and, as with the division between individualistic and collectivist cultures (see Myth 2), there is a continuum. For example, North Americans, who are generally classified as low contact, are notably more high contact than the low-contact cultures of Scandinavia, yet very much less so than the Latin American high-contact cultures (Andersen et al., 2003). In addition, there are important gender differences within and across cultures (Dibiase & Gunnoe, 2004; Semnani-Azad & Adair, 2011)

Let's look at some specific non-verbal behaviors and the research.

Gestures

Certain symbolic gestures, also known as *emblematic* gestures, are the most obvious type of non-verbal communication. Research over many decades has explored emblematic gestures and their different meanings in various cultures, (e.g., Safadi & Valentine, 1988; Kendon, 2004; Kirch, 1979). Two common examples of such gestures used in the U.S. are using hands/fingers to indicate OK and "thumbs up." The OK symbol is formed by joining one's first finger and thumb. For "thumbs up," Americans close the other fingers so that only the thumb is pointing up. These symbols are used in movies, on TV shows, in business settings, on the street, etc., with no problem, until the gesture is viewed by someone from a culture where this emblematic gesture has a different meaning. In Brazil, for instance, the U.S. OK symbol is an obscene gesture, and in Arab countries, giving the thumbs up is similar to the North American "middle finger."

As a result, it is better not to use gestures in another country unless you are very sure that you are conveying what you mean. It's all too easy to overlook a minor but essential detail. In 1992 then U.S. President George Bush notoriously offered an insult to Australians when he made a gesture by spreading his index finger and second finger into a "V" with his palm facing inward. In the U.S., this gesture, regardless of palm position, indicates "peace," or in an older meaning, "victory." In Australia, as well as other parts of the U.K., the inward-facing palm gesture is the equivalent of offering someone once again, "the middle finger."

Eye Contact

Eye contact or gaze can lead to very different interpretations of intent. As indicated by the In the Real World story, in the U.S., speakers expect eye contact to last about a second, and then people glance away, glance back, and repeat the cycle (Burgoon, Guerrero,

& Floyd, 2010). When this does not occur, Americans feel there is something "off" because they are not receiving the expected feedback: Is the other person not listening, being disrespectful, or ignoring me? Yet other cultures use eye contact differently as shown in the In the Real World story of the Latina student in the principal's office. Similary, in most Asian, sub-Saharan, and Arab cultures, not looking someone in the eye if that person is of higher status, older, in a position of authority, or of the opposite sex shows respect and does not indicate inattention (Akechi et al., 2013; Richmond & Gestrin, 2009; Samarah, 2015).

Space

Differences in non-verbal behaviors are related to notions of personal space, or the invisible "bubble" people like to have around them. Many of us have probably experienced the "conversation dance." Here, speakers have a different interpretation of how close is too close when speaking with someone else. For Americans, it's about "an arm's length" away from each other (Knapp, Hall, & Horgan, 2013). Anything closer can result in one person starting to move away from the other. This action, when the other person is a member of a culture that prefers less distance between speakers, can cause awkwardness, even causing one person to keep moving closer while the other tries to increase the distance/space. This type of behavior is famously illustrated in two *Seinfeld* episodes (Season 5, Episodes 18–19), an American sitcom (1989–1998), where Jerry Seinfeld coins the term *close talker* to refer to someone who invades another person's personal space. In these episodes, the character breaks the (unwritten) rules of personal space with humorous results.

Low-contact cultures such as the U.S. prefer greater personal space; high-contact cultures less so. As I was writing this book, I had an appointment at a doctor's office. What struck me about the waiting room was how people spread themselves in the chairs as far apart from one another as possible and no one interacted with anyone else. The only exceptions were those people who came in with a companion. As more people came in, and by necessity had to start filling in more of the chairs, I noticed how people maintained their personal space by not looking at others, and, as soon as chairs became vacant, moved away from one another. Ümit, a Turkish colleague, noted that in Turkey, in contrast, women prefer to sit close to another woman rather then spread out as they wait for an appointment, even if the space is big because they feel more comfortable. Kenneth, a Taiwanese colleague, described how in Taiwan people will choose seats in a waiting room close to someone else, rather than spread out because they prefer to be close to others. And both Kenneth and Ümit remarked that in doctors' waiting rooms, older people frequently strike up conversations with other patients whom they don't know to share their health concerns and potential cures, remedies, and options.

This preference for more personal space also manifests itself on public transportation. When you enter a bus without many people, do you choose to sit next to someone or choose a seat alone? When there are three people on a subway train sitting in a row and the person at the end leaves at the next stop, do you move down so that there is an empty seat between you and the other rider, or do you stay where you are? While of course there are personal preferences involved, overall our reactions have to do with whether or not we are members of cultures that prefer a greater or smaller personal bubble. In the U.S., people tend to prefer more personal space and will generally chose the seat alone and move to the empty seat. A completely "normal" practice in the U.S., this can be construed as "rude" in other cultures, such as Spain or Ecuador where there are different notions of personal space.

U.S. teachers may also find themselves engaged in the "conversational dance" when speaking with students or their family members who have other interpretations of personal space. And, in classroom settings, students may have different notions of what constitutes personal space. U.S. students tend to be possessive of their personal bubble and often feel uncomfortable when students from other cultures "crowd" them by sitting or moving closer during conversations or group activities than the Americans are used to. At the same time, the other students may feel that Americans are standoffish and distant because of their preference for a greater personal bubble.

Contact

Touching or contact behaviors also differ cross-culturally. Cultures differ in whether they encourage or permit touching behaviors such as hugging, kissing, or walking hand-in-hand. At times teachers and administrators hear complaints from families from cultures where public displays of affection between males and females are frowned upon or forbidden because their children are exposed to this type of behavior among students in U.S. schools.

High-contact cultures such as Latin American, southern and eastern European, and Arab cultures prefer more touching behaviors than do Asian and northern European cultures (Andersen et al., 2003), although there are gender, intimacy, and situational differences (Samover, Porter, & McDaniel, 2014).

In many Latin American cultures, such as Guatemala, Ecuador, or Brazil, women may walk arm-in-arm or hold hands with another woman and men may do the same as a sign of friendship (Flaitz, 2006). Arm- and handholding as well as other public displays of affection occur publicly between men and women. In Arab cultures, men may walk hand-in-hand as a sign of deep friendship, but never a woman and a man (Nydell, 2012).

Contact behaviors between adults and children are in many ways culturally influenced. Ana, in the U.S. studying for her

Master's in TESOL, was struck by what she saw as the lack of close contact between her children and their teachers, compared to in her home country, Chile:

> Teachers always hug the young children and they often sit on their laps. Here, when my son is sad, the teacher gives him maybe a quick hug, maybe not. And in my daughter's second grade, there is no hugging, nothing. I understand why it's different here but the children, they miss it.

Emotions

Emotions are also often expressed non-verbally. Cultures differ as to whether feelings may be expressed publicly and to what degree or how intensely these emotions may be expressed. In Asian cultures, with their emphasis on relationships and harmony, it is considered more polite to keep one's feelings to oneself in order to avoid hurting or distressing others (Matsumoto, 2006). The Japanese, for instance, are culturally conditioned to mask their emotions (Jack et al., 2009; Yuki, Maddux, & Matsuda, 2007). On the other hand, Latin American cultures highly value emotional expressiveness (Scollon et al., 2004). Rather than underplaying their emotions when they are feeling happy, for instance, members of Latin American cultures are comfortable with overt emotional displays, although public displays of anger are generally frowned up (Flaitz, 2006; Ruby et al., 2012).

In some cases, when students from cultures that traditionally keep emotions to themselves have outbursts or other overt emotional displays, this can be a sign of post-traumatic stress disorder (PTSD) (Hos, 2014). In such cases, students should be referred to appropriate social services for evaluation and counseling.

Silence

Another area often discussed in conjunction with non-verbal communication is silence (see also Myth 3). When is it appropriate to be silent and when does one speak up? English has the adage "Silence is golden," but how can we have silence and a conversation? Aren't the terms *silence* and *conversation* contradictory? Isn't the point of conversation to talk? The answer to these questions is, from the U.S. point of view, yes. And when Americans do encounter silence in conversational settings, they tend to be uncomfortable. For speakers in other cultures, there is the sense that silence is part of the conversation, allowing a person to reflect, to focus, or to gather one's thoughts before actually saying something (Brislin & Kim, 2003). In the U.S., speakers generally don't wait for long pauses to enter a conversation after one speaker has finished. If no one jumps in right away to carry on the conversation, there is the sense that there is something wrong. Chinese, for instance, do not "jump" into a conversation; they wait for their turn. While they wait, they indicate they are listening by keeping both their voice and their body still (Meyer, 2014). This stillness, from the U.S. perspective, signals taciturnity and even disengagement rather than attention.

Non-Verbal Communication and the Classroom

Non-verbal communication is, in so many ways, a hidden language (Hall, 1966, 1984)—that is, we don't know we "speak" it until we encounter situations in which we don't understand the silent message being conveyed or someone misunderstands what we were trying to communicate. In the classroom, too, different patterns of non-verbal communication between students and teachers can cause misunderstandings. Students from different cultural backgrounds may have different comfort levels with the expressiveness of teachers' non-verbal behaviors (Georgakopoulous & Guerrero, 2010). A study by Orton (2006) illustrates differing expectations of non-verbal behaviors. Australian respondents reacted negatively to Chinese speakers' "stillness of body and hands" (p. 302), while the Chinese felt that speakers' appropriate non-verbal behavior included erect posture with only a few circumscribed gestures at times.

Another question to ponder is what is appropriate listening posture? Today, for most U.S. teachers, if students slouch, cross their legs, or sprawl in their seats but maintain eye contact, then the non-verbal communication is not particularly significant. However, in other cultures, sitting up straight while keeping one's eyes closed and the head turned upward indicates listening (Damen, 1987). In Muslim cultures, crossing one's leg and directing the sole of one's shoe toward another person is insulting, regardless of the type (or lack) of eye contact. In Haiti, it is considered a sign of respect for students to stand with their arms crossed and look down when addressing a teacher (Shoorman & Velouse, 2003).

Because non-verbal aspects are such an integral part of communication, teachers and students need to become aware of differences between their non-verbal behaviors and those of the target language (Orton, 2006). Non-verbal behaviors are open to considerable misinterpretation unless the cultural context and code are shared. However, learning to understand a different culture's norms and forms of non-verbal communication is not an easy process (Soudek & Soudek, 1985; Witte, 2011, 2014). This is because, as already noted, it is not a type of communication that is necessarily obvious because we engage in it subconsciously. Much of our non-verbal behaviors are ingrained and difficult for us to change, even when we know there are differences. As an American student who had spent time in Bulgaria once put it:

> You're in a country where shaking your head means yes and nodding your head means no, just the opposite of the U.S. You know this, you've been told this, you've seen it, but then you're in a store checking out and the cashier asks you if you want a bag. What do you do? You nod your head. What hap-

pens? You don't get the bag and then you suddenly realize that once again, you "said" the opposite of what you meant because you automatically responded without paying very careful attention and doing the opposite of what you were used to.

Many teachers of international students have commented that they have learned not to ask "Do you understand?" because the head nod they receive in response to this question does not indicate yes. In many Asian cultures, nodding one's head means, "Yes, I heard you" and not "I understand what you said." Neither action or interpretation is in and of itself incorrect, but examples of different norms governing the appropriate response to someone in a position of authority. In the U.S., admitting that you didn't understand is acceptable because teachers expect students to let them know when and how they need help. From the Korean or Chinese perspective, explicitly admitting you need help could cause teachers to lose face because it would imply that they were not good teachers. Even when students become aware of the different expectations their teachers have of the head nod, they find it difficult to answer no to such a question. From the Asian perspective no is very direct and potentially face-threatening in that it can imply that the teachers failed in their instruction (Ting-Toomey & Chung, 2012).

In addition to the difficulty of changing one's non-verbal behaviors, non-verbal communication is not generally part of the language learning curriculum, apart from a few general comments about common emblematic gestures. Awareness and understanding of underlying reasons for differing cultural concepts of non-verbal behavior does not automatically occur by traveling or living in another country but through conscious examination and reflection (Corder & U-Mackey, 2015). Some explicit attention to non-verbal behavior should be taught in the classroom.

What We Can Do . . .

1. Ask students to share information about non-verbal behaviors of their cultures.

Since so much of our non-verbal communication is unconscious, set the stage for the students. Provide examples, visually or written, of how things are done in the U.S. and ask them to discuss what might be done differently in their cultures and why. For example, show

- a meal around a table where someone is handing another person a utensil or dish with the left hand
  - Is it acceptable to use the left hand to hand someone something? If not, why not?
  - How close are people sitting?
- an adult patting or touching a child's head
  - Is it inappropriate to pat a child's head? (In Buddhist cultures, the head is viewed as the home of the soul.)
- a man and a woman shaking hands or one touching the other casually on the shoulder
  - Is mixed-gender handshaking common?
  - Is touching someone on the shoulder an invasion of personal space or a simple way to get someone's attention?
  - Might this be permissible between people of the same gender but not between a male and female?

2. Discuss what non-verbal behaviors constitute part of greeting and leaving-taking rituals.

Explore different ways people greet each other and say goodbye. Students from diverse cultures or who have lived overseas can share what they are familiar with or have experienced. There are also many examples of greeting and leave-taking rituals found on YouTube by searching "greetings cross-culturally" or "saying good-bye cross-culturally."

Topics for discussion include:

- In some cultures, people bow as part of the greeting ritual.
  - Do they bow with their whole body?
  - Do people just bow their heads?
  - What role do the hands play?
  - Are there differences in bowing behaviors depending on status, age, and/or gender?
- In other cultures, people shake hands as they greet one another and again as they say goodbye.
  - Do they shake hands in all contexts? If not, in which types of contexts? Do, for instance, teachers and parents shake hands? What about teachers and students?
  - Are there gender and status differences in handshaking behavior?
- In some cultures, do students greet their teachers at the beginning of the school day or a class by standing up?
- In some cultures, do students and teachers bow to each other when they see each other outside of the classroom?
- In some cultures, do children in primary grades chant in unison a version of "Good morning, teacher" as they remain seated?

Ask students to consider why these behaviors differ? What cultural values do they reflect?

3. Learn about common non-verbal dos and taboos across cultures.

There are many lists of basic dos and taboos available on the internet. If you can't find the particular cultures your students may come from, can you extrapolate knowing what you do know? For example, Muslims regard the left hand as unclean and should not be used for handing something to someone. If you have Muslim students from a country in central Africa about which you can't find much information, you can still assume that you should not give them anything with your left hand.

Share some of these dos and taboos with your students. What are their reactions? What others can they add? Can they explain where they might stem from? What are some examples in the U.S? How do they compare to those in other countries?

4. Develop greater awareness of what constitutes "personal space."

A fun activity to develop awareness of people's unconscious practice of personal space is based on Edward T. Hall's groundbreaking work on personal space or proxemics (1966, 1984). In a building with an elevator, ask students to observe people's behavior:

- Do people move away from each other as they enter the elevator?
- When the elevator is empty except for you, where do you choose to stand? What happens when one other person enters the elevator on another floor and there are now two of you?
- When the elevator is relatively empty, does one person move into the corner while the next person moves into the opposite corner?

- Which way are people facing in the elevator? What are people's reactions if you face the opposite way?
- What kind of eye contact do you notice?
- If the elevator is crowded, how do people protect their personal space?

Alternatively, ask students to observe people's personal space behavior in a waiting room, dining hall, or on public transportation. Ask them to describe what cultural, ethnic, and/or gender differences they notice.

Note: You may want to introduce the elevator activity by viewing a video on personal space in elevators. Videos can be found on the internet by searching "elevator" and "personal space."

5. Make use of media to explore non-verbal communication.

An effective and popular activity for exploring non-verbal communication is to watch short but illustrative movie or TV clips without sound. The internet has compilations from popular TV series such as *Friends* or *I Love Lucy*. You can choose to focus on one element of non-verbal communication or on several different ones, depending on the clip you select, the proficiency level of your students, and their cultural backgrounds. You may want to start with aspects of non-verbal behaviors you have noticed that differ among your students and those in the U.S. As they watch, ask students to take notes or complete a simple activity sheet like the Sample Observation Chart to use for later discussion or a writing assignment.

Sample Observation Chart: Gestures
Brief description of the context:
Description of participants (e.g., same sex, woman-man, older-younger, friends, strangers, etc.):
Part of body involved (e.g., hand, whole body):
What happened?

See DeCapua & Wintergerst (2016), pages 191–195, "Observation Protocol," for additional suggestions and examples.

6. Ask students to make short videos illustrating non-verbal behaviors.

Students may choose to make videos showing humorous examples of cultural misunderstandings or straightforward factual videos. Caution students to avoid stereotyping or only illustrating superficial elements of non-verbal communication. Samples can be found on the internet, but not all are of equal quality. One good example is the close talker *Seinfeld* episodes mentioned in this chapter. Another example is *The Office: Pitching to Women* (Season 9, Episode 7).

The movie *Freaky Friday* demonstrates how non-verbal behaviors reveal much about a person's age and social role. In the movie, the mother, Tess, and her teenage daughter, Anna, wake up one morning to discover that they are inhabiting each other's bodies. Although they have switched bodies, Tess and Anna maintain their own age and role body language.

And finally, the TV series *The Big Bang Theory* has various episodes on non-verbal communication. These can be located by using the search terms "body language" or "non-verbal communication" together with *The Big Bang Theory*.

MYTH 5

How something is said is not as important as what is said.

In the Real World . . .

One of my German cousins, Eva, and I decided to take a cross-country trip across the U.S about 12 years ago. We started in New York City and made our way very leisurely to the West Coast. After many miles, many sights, and various adventures, it was time for us to head back. At this point, we were somewhat pressed for time because Eva had to catch her flight back to Germany, so Eva and I switched off driving after each tank of gas, with no plans to stop again until New York. At one point late at night, it was Eva's turn and I took the opportunity to nap. She was driving on an empty stretch of the interstate in Texas, doing well over the speed limit, when suddenly out of nowhere she heard the wailing of a police car. Once Eva realized that the police car was coming after our car, she slowed down and pulled over. When the police officer approached, she rolled down the window. I woke up just as he asked her, "Ma'am, do you have a driver's license?" Eva replied,

"Of course." He looked at her, and said, "Do you mind giving it to me?" She gave him her license, he wrote her a ticket, and we went on our way.

Several things have always struck me about Eva and the police officer's exchange. For one, I could tell by the officer's body language that how Eva uttered "of course" offended him. It was not an "American" "of course" appropriate for this situation.

"Of course" was all she said; she didn't expand by adding something along the lines of, "Of course, it's right here in my purse" or "Of course, let me get it out." By providing additional information, Eva would have sent a different message. Moreover, given the context, it might have been better if Eva would have not used "of course" at all, but perhaps, "Yes, sir." Eva's story illustrates how communicating the intended message in another language is not as easy as using the right words.

Another example relates to making the wrong word or vocabulary choices even when there is a one-to-one correspondence between two languages. English has the modal verbs *must* and *should*, and German has *müssen* and *sollen* (for "must" and "should"). One would likely therefore think that one could translate either verb easily from one language to the other and vice versa. This is actually not always correct because these verbs belong to what linguists call different *semantic fields*. In other words, although there is a one-to-one corresponding translation, when and how these two verbs are used differs in the two languages.

In my work on complaints produced by Americans and German learners of English, I found that the Germans frequently used *must* in situations where Americans would use *should* (DeCapua, 1998). The result of the inappropriate use of *must* influenced the Americans in evaluating the Germans as rude and abrasive. The intended meaning is the same, but the choice of *should* over *must* communicates a somewhat different message. In American English, *must* conveys the idea of necessity or obligation, but Americans will often use *should* to convey this meaning instead of *must*. Using *should* in place of *must* "softens" an utterance, making it sound less demanding or harsh even though it is conveying the idea that the "suggestion" is really a demand or obligation (DeCapua, 2017). This use is illustrated, for instance, on the *TESOL Quarterly* website where the instructions for authors state that "[a]ll submissions to *TQ* should conform to the requirements of . . ." (*TESOL Quarterly* submission guidelines).

Another example of the incorrect use of *must* is its use by many English learners, as in "Teacher, you must help me" or "Teacher, you must understand my problem." The students are unintentionally demanding rather than requesting, which can annoy or even anger teachers unaware of such language learner matters.

Another example of the difficulty of communicating one's intended message in another language concerns directness. How direct or indirect a message is conveyed depends on the language and culture. In some cultures, such as in the U.S., speakers employ a direct communication style, meaning that whatever words they say convey the entirety of the message. They say (more or less) what they think and their words are to be interpreted literally (again, more or less). Having said this, speakers do use indirect speech acts, particularly when being polite. By indirect speech acts, we mean that speakers use alternative speech forms to convey something else than what the form itself suggests (Eckert & McConnell-Ginet, 2003). In other words, the implicit meaning is the intended meaning, not the words themselves. For example, "Can you open the window?" or "Could you pass me the salt?" is not really a question about one's ability to do either task, but a polite request to someone to do something.

In other cultures, speakers prefer more indirect communication styles, where the meaning is even less explicitly stated. Thus, interactions between U.S. educators and families from diverse cultural and linguistic backgrounds can be challenging (Cheatham

& Santos, 2011; Ramirez, 2003). For example, in some cultures, refusals are hinted at rather than expressed and the subtext is as important as the words. Recall the Japanese businessman (Myth 4).

Consider this exchange between an American teacher and a Chinese parent:

> Teacher (calling child's home, reaches the mother): *Hello, Mrs. Chan. I'm calling to see if I can set up a meeting with the school counselor, Mrs. Rodriguez, you and your husband, and me about Kuan-Chi next Wednesday evening. If you can come, I'll block out the time and let Mrs. Rodriguez know.*
>
> Mrs. Chan: *It is possible that my husband will have to travel then.*
>
> (3 days later)
>
> Teacher (calling again): *Hello, Mrs. Chan. I'm following up to see whether you and your husband will be able to come for a conference on Wednesday as we discussed.*
>
> Mrs. Chan: (silence, thinking to herself, "But I told her no").

What we see here is a cultural difference in communication styles. For Mrs. Chan, she indicated "no" indirectly in a way appropriate in Chinese culture by offering an excuse that she prefaced with the non-committal phrase "It is possible . . . ." Mrs. Chan expected that the teacher would read between the lines and understand that she meant no. From the Chinese viewpoint, a vague or non-committal phrase allows speakers to indirectly refuse a request they cannot or do not want to fulfill (Pan, 2012). To say no explicitly would have been rude. For the American teacher, in contrast, an explicit response, either a yes or a no (with a reason why) would have been appropriate and would not have caused offense. Direct refusals, as long as they are accompanied by a plausible reason for the refusal, are not construed as rude or face-threatening to Americans (Beebe & Takahashi, 1989; Félix-Brasdefer, 2008).

This conversation between Mrs. Chan and the teacher shows how two speakers from different cultures used different communication styles, which led to a misunderstanding. When we consider what each speaker said and expected, we can attribute much of this to differences in high-context versus low-context cultures (Hall, 1966). In *high-context* cultures, which are often cultures with much ethnic homogeneity and a long, shared history, little needs to be said because much or most of speakers' intended meaning can be gleaned from context. Because messages tend to be communicated within the framework of a shared code of (mostly) unwritten rules, speakers avoid confrontation and loss to a person's face, just like Mrs. Chan's "It is possible." Saying no or giving a direct refusal can be construed as impolite and face-threatening so speakers employ subtle hints and non-verbal cues instead (Gudykunst & Kim, 2003). *Low-context* cultures such as the U.S. and Canada are more heterogeneous with a strong history of immigration, so there is less of a shared, implicit code among speakers; thus, the emphasis is on clarity and explicitness so that hearers will understand messages. Thus, indirect communication, such as Mrs. Chan's, is only effective when speakers share the code, which was not the case with Mrs. Chan and the American teacher.

What the Research Says . . .

For several decades, there has been great interest in understanding how speakers use language to convey meaning and understanding when breakdowns or miscommunications occur across cultures (e.g., Bardovi-Harlig & Hartford, 2005; Blum-Kulka, House, & Kasper, 1989; Trosberg, 2010). This area of language study is referred to as *pragmatics.* Speakers' ability to use and understand language effectively in natural contexts is referred to as *pragmatic competence* and their inability to do so as *pragmatic failure* (Thomas, 1983). As we saw in the interaction with Mrs. Chan, pragmatic failure occurred because she was using the indirectness norms of her native language when speaking English with her child's American teacher.

Conversational Routines

In addition to different norms of directness, different cultures and languages have varying routines for everyday social interactions. These routines are known as *conversational routines.* They provide structure and help maintain culturally appropriate conversational interactions. Everyday conversation routines may be easily recognized and learned by language learners, but this does not mean that they always comprehend their function. A common complaint from language learners about Americans is that they are superficial or false, as in this common example: "In greeting someone Americans ask, 'How are you?' but then they don't listen when we tell them!" The reason this example is so frequently cited is because "How are you?" in this context is part of a conversational routine, not an actual, informational question that requires an answer. Americans expect a standard response as part of this greeting routine, or "script," such as "Fine, thanks" or "Not bad, and you?" People from other cultures may not realize that this question is part of the greeting script rather than the beginning of a conversation about one's health (DeCapua & Wintergerst, 2016).

All cultures have their own greeting routines. The Chinese, for example, ask, "Have you eaten?" and the Koreans "Have you eaten rice today?" In neither case do speakers expect a truthful answer. These Chinese and Korean greeting routines will be confusing to the American who thinks either one of these greetings is a "real" question rather than understanding it as a greeting routine.

It is not only essential to know the routine or script, but it's also necessary to know the use of different options when they exist.

Different contexts require different routines. For instance, greeting someone with "Hi" or "Hello, how are you?" are only two of the ways to greet someone in the U.S. Another greeting that language learners frequently pick up is the casual greeting, "What's up?" (generally pronounced to sound like "Whassup"). Once learners know this form, they frequently use it inappropriately because they don't realize that its use is generally restricted to friends, close family members, and peers. Using "What's up?" with teachers, administrators, or someone who has a higher status or who is older is generally evaluated negatively—that is, the speaker is viewed as being disrespectful. Learning the different ways to greet and respond to greetings based on the situation and context can be complex for students to learn.

Another type of interactional routine relates to leave-taking. When Americans say goodbye, they often include phrases such as, "See you soon" or "Let's have lunch sometime." To other ears, these phrases seem like real promises or invitations when, from the American perspective, they are simply part of the friendly leave-taking routine using what Wolfson (1989) calls *pseudo-invitations*. The message behind these types of statements is to demonstrate friendliness or rapport, not to extend an actual invitation. To members of other cultures with different routines and norms, such statements are easily misinterpreted and taken at face value (Shapiro et al., 2014). Some Americans may have experienced the awkward situation where the intended meaning was not understood by a non-native speaker. I remember one incident very clearly where in saying goodbye to an international graduate student at the end of the semester I included, "You'll have to come by and visit some time." I then found the person unexpectedly at my door the following week, along with his wife and young toddler.

Another difference in leave-taking is the length of time it takes to say goodbye. Americans generally keep it short: If a group of casual friends is saying goodbye, they might say, for instance, "Bye, see you soon," perhaps including a wave or perhaps not; this will be understood as saying goodbye to everyone who is present. In other cultures, this type of minimal leave-taking would be considered rude. For example, in Colombia, speakers have to address everyone explicitly, kiss everyone on the cheek as appropriate, and repeat the goodbye for several rounds before actually leaving. In Germany, leave-taking is not as extensive as in Colombia, but speakers, even young people, generally include a handshake as they address each person with "goodbye."

Classroom teachers have described how difficult they sometimes find it to end meetings with parents from Latino and sub-Saharan African cultures because the leave-taking routines and cues differ from those in the U.S. One student, Monica, wrote about this in her journal:

> It was getting late and I really needed to leave to pick up my son from daycare, but the mother, she was from Somalia, just wanted to talk, and talk, and talk. And it had nothing to do with school. I kept trying to say things like, "Well, it's been good talking with you" or "It's getting late"; I packed up all my things, closed my bag, and put on my coat, but she never got the hint. I finally had to say, "I'm glad we had the chance to talk, but I have to leave right now to get my son. Goodbye!" And then I walked out. I know she wasn't happy but she just didn't get that I was trying to end the conversation. This to me was a classic case of when we talked about pragmatic failure!

Speech Acts

Greeting and parting rituals are just two examples of the many daily conversational routines that everyone engages in and thinks little about that are governed by implicit cultural norms (see Myth 3). In following cultural norms, speakers may employ specific types of utterances. Because of this fact, it can be difficult to realize what purpose these routines have and how they reflect certain norms.

Utterances that serve specific communicative functions are called *speech acts;* examples are apologizing, making requests, or giving advice. Speech acts and how they are realized by first language speakers, by learners of a second language, or in contrast from one language to another, is one of the most researched areas in pragmatics. Table 5.1 offers a small sample of cross-cultural studies on the topic of speech acts.

Some researchers argue that to better understand how speakers communicate, the focus should be on the discourse level, not on individual speech acts and the utterance level. Considering the structure or "big picture" of a conversation allows us to investigate in greater depth questions such as: How do people take turns in a conversation? How do they move from one topic to another? What contextual and situational factors (e.g., age, social status, familiarity) influence turn-taking and moves? What kinds of strategies do speakers engage in (Huth & Taleghani-Nikzam, 2006)? How do speakers convey and interpret politeness (Harris, 2001)? What are the cultural norms underlying politeness and how do speakers show politeness?

Politeness

Brown and Levinson, early and very influential researchers in this area (1978, 1987), proposed that speakers want to maintain *face* (Goffman, 1972) or their personal self-image with respect to others; they also proposed that interactions that jeopardize this self-image are *face-threatening acts*, so speakers engage in negative and positive strategies, or *face-saving acts*, in conversational interactions to maintain face. To maintain face, speakers use politeness strategies, like the indirect speech acts mentioned earlier: "Could you pass me the salt?"

Interpretations of politeness and associated language use vary substantially. It's not just *what* you say that's important, but how and in which context. Through the socialization or enculturation process of becoming an adult member of a culture (see Myth 1),

Table 5.1: Cross-Cultural Studies on Speech Acts

Speech Act	Researcher(s)	Study[1]
Giving advice	Chentsova-Dutton & Vaughn (2011)	Compares advice among Americans, Russians, and Russian-Americans
	DeCapua & Dunham (2007)	Looks at advice-giving among native speakers of American English, advanced learners of English, and highly proficient/near-native speakers of English
	Limburg & Locher (2012)	Examines giving advice with diverse speakers in a variety of settings, including online, face-to-face, and in writing
Apologizing	Barnlund & Yoshioka (1990)	Compares apologies in American English and Japanese
	Bataineh & Bataineh (2008)	Reports results on apologies as produced by native speakers of American English and Jordanian Arabic
	Blum-Kulka, House, & Kasper (1989)	Investigates Hebrew, Danish, German, Canadian French, British, American, and Australian English apologies, as well as requests
Complaining	Chen, Chen, & Chang (2011)	Examines complaints by American English and Taiwanese Chinese speakers
	Eslami-Rasekh (2005)	Considers how American and Persian speakers react to and respond to complaints
	Murphy & Neu (1996)	Reports on complaints by native speakers of American English and Korean non-native speakers of English
Giving compliments	Chen (2010)	Provides overview of research on complimenting in various languages, including Irish English, Polish, Chinese, Japanese, Turkish, Persian, and Arabic, among others
	Maíz-Arévalo (2012)	Compares implicit compliments in English and Spanish
	Yu (2011)	Contrasts complimenting by native speakers of American English and Taiwanese Chinese

[1] Some of these studies examine more than one speech act.

Table 5.1 (continued): Cross-Cultural Studies on Speech Acts

Speech Act	Researcher(s)	Study[1]
Expressing gratitude	Eisenstein & Bodman (1986)	Considers the act of thanking someone between native speakers of American English and Japanese learners of English
	Özdemir & Rezvani (2010)	Looks at expressions of thanks by Turkish and Iranian learners of English and native English speakers
	Park & Lee (2012)	Explores thanking by Koreans and Americans
Refusing	Beebe, Takahashi, & Uliss-Weltz (1990)	Examines refusals by Japanese learners of English
	Félix-Brasdefer (2008)	Compares refusals among speakers of Mexican, Costa Rican, and Dominican Republic Spanish
	Kwon (2004)	Discusses refusals by natives speakers of Korean versus native speakers of American English
	Morkus (2014)	Contrasts refusals by speakers of Egyptian Arabic and American English
Making requests	Byon (2004)	Reports on requests by Americans learning Korean as a foreign language
	Pinto & Raschio (2007)	Investigates requests by heritage speakers of Spanish, Mexican native speakers of Spanish, and native speakers of American English
	Reiter (2002)	Compares requests between Spanish speakers from Spain and Uruguay

[1] Some of these studies examine more than one speech act.

individuals learn what can or cannot be said, how it can be said, and how messages, both verbal and non-verbal, are to be interpreted (DeCapua & Wintergerst, 2016). In other words, everyone develops pragmatic competence, at least to some degree, within their own culture. However, when we interact with members of other cultures, varying notions of pragmatic competences may be present, leading to the kinds of cross-cultural misunderstandings that we often hear about and experience ourselves (Beal, 1992; Rose & Kasper, 2001).

This chapter gave the example of a cross-cultural misunderstanding in the conversations between the American teacher and Mrs. Chan. And, when cross-cultural misunderstandings result, speakers tend to assign negative traits or evaluations to the other because they are reacting to the communication based on the norms of their own language and culture: "He didn't apologize, so he's a rude person" or "The teachers don't really care. They never want to talk about us and our families" or "Why can't they ever tell the truth?" (Cheatham & Santos, 2011).

In addition, indirect speech act use by teachers can be confusing to learners who don't understand the implicit meaning. For example, in written feedback, teachers write questions such as, "Can you give an example here?" However, learners frequently don't realize that the question is, in fact, asking them to do something. It is an indirect request or command to the student to add something to their written work (Ferris, 2007; Ferris & Hedgcock, 2013). As Baker and Bricker (2010) note, students need to be able to accurately interpret teacher feedback to be able to correct problems.

In short, pragmatic competence, or the appropriate use of language, is an important feature of language learning. Although this is true for all language learners, it is particularly necessary for those who live, study, and/or work in a country where there is one primary or official language and where they will be interacting frequently with native speakers.

Teaching Pragmatics

Students do not necessarily learn the pragmatics of a new language without instruction (Bardovi-Harlig, 2001; Taguchi, 2015). In developing pragmatic competence, non-native speakers must understand—at a deep level—both the language and the culture (Ishihara & Cohen, 2010). Sharifian and Jamarani (2011) describe a situation in which a highly proficient Iranian student prefaces her thanks to her U.S. instructor who had written her a letter of recommendation with, "I'm ashamed." The instructor is confused by this statement and wonders what the student has done because if it had been said by an American student, it would mean the student has done something wrong. The miscommunication is a result of what appears to the instructor to be an apology but that is, for the Iranian student, the proper way to express thanks when someone has done that person an important favor. Despite her advanced language proficiency, the Iranian student was not aware of the differing pragmatics of thanking and how her language use would be interpreted by a native speaker of American English.

One major challenge in teaching pragmatics is knowing what one's own pragmatic rules are, how they might differ across languages and cultures, and how to go about sharing this knowledge with learners. Features of one's own language and use are difficult to understand through introspection alone (Wolfson, 1989). What native speakers think they say does not necessarily match what they really say or think others actually say (Golato, 2005). Vásquez and Fioramonte (2011) describe how surprised an American graduate student was by the results of her research project on requests in a Master's in TESOL course. The student had expected that older speakers would use *please* significantly more than would younger speakers in making requests. Her expectation, however, did not align with her research findings. There was no difference between older and younger speakers in their use of *please*, contrary to what the graduate student believed to be the case.

While there has been an increasing amount of research in pragmatics, particularly on speech acts and politeness, the number of empirical studies is still limited, and research that has been conducted and published is not always accessible to those without a linguistics, particularly sociolinguistics, background. Pragmatic awareness requires training and practice, yet few TESOL Methods courses place much emphasis on *teaching* the pragmatics of language (Vásquez & Fioramonte, 2011). This means that it may not be clear to new ESL teachers what they should do in their classrooms. And if they do want to talk about it in the classroom, what material do they use? How accurate is the pragmatic information presented in language textbooks? How applicable is it to the real world?

Currently, textbook presentations of pragmatic information leave much to be desired, both for their superficial presentation of routines and linguistic forms and their tendency to overgeneralize the use and applicability of these routines/norms (Ishihara & Cohen, 2010; McConachy & Hata, 2013). There has been much discussion of this, particularly in English textbooks published internationally or locally where English is not the primary language of the country. Ren & Zheng (2016) found that English language textbooks in China, when they did include pragmatic information, tended to simplify speech acts to a few basic patterns. In instances where the textbooks offered various possible responses when thanking someone, for example, they did not include any, or only limited, information as to which response would be (more) appropriate in a given context. Even when a textbook did make mention of classifying possible responses based on formality, there was no discussion of why one possibility would be considered more formal than another. In another study of textbooks, Meihami and Khanlarzadeh (2015) reported that the strategies speakers engage in when requesting, refusing, and most especially, apologizing were oversimplified, whether the books were published internationally or locally.

Despite these issues and concerns, explicit instruction is crucial since non-native speakers do not necessarily pick up the pragmatics of their new language (Bardovi-Harlig, 2012; Frenz-Belkin, 2015).

Using authentic materials as examples and models, teachers can incorporate pragmatics in their instruction to help students recognize which areas are likely to cause misunderstandings on the road to becoming more successful communicators in their new language. To help teachers to do so, efforts have been made to develop instructional methods, lesson plans, and teaching suggestions on pragmatics, and teachers now have some good resources available to them, particularly for speech acts (see Taguchi 2011; 2015, for discussion and review). Ishihara and Cohen (2010), for example, discuss how to assess pragmatic information in textbooks and adapt and design instruction.

There are also high-quality websites with information on teaching pragmatics. The Center for Advanced Research on Language Acquisition (CARLA) at the University of Minnesota, for instance, provides both research and information on teaching pragmatics, not only in English but also in various other languages. This website can be located by searching "CARLA" and "pragmatics" or "CARLA" and "University of Minnesota." Another website is americanenglish.state.gov. This is a forum for English language teachers globally with many practical suggestions and activities for teaching pragmatics. On this website is an article by Hillard (2017) that provides activities for teaching the speech act of complaining. Also available is an article by Siegel with activities on apologizing and requesting. The website can be found be searching "American English Teaching."

What We Can Do . . .

1. Evaluate your students' receptive language skills.

How much pragmatic knowledge are they ready for as they struggle to learn the basics of the new language? Are they at a low level of language proficiency and would benefit most from learning common routines? Or are they at an advanced level where they would benefit from identifying the cultural norms underlying communicative interactions? Once you have evaluated their skills, consider using some of the resources increasingly available for building students' pragmatic knowledge, from, for instance, the Center for Advanced Research on Language Acquisition (CARLA), or using a text such as Ishihara and Cohen's (2010) to guide you in designing your own instruction.

2. Look for teachable moments about pragmatics.

If a student greets you when entering the classroom with "What's up" or "Hey," use this as an opportunity for all students to practice appropriate greetings in different contexts. Also, many U.S. teachers, when addressed as "Teacher," react negatively to being referred to with this word. They consider it silly (e.g., being called by their profession), rude, or discourteous. If this happens, discuss how teachers and professors prefer to be addressed and how this may differ in different educational settings (K–12, adult education, or university). If a student enters the class late and tries to greet you and all the other students individually rather than quietly taking a seat, take this as an opportunity to discuss classroom routines, and differences depending on whether the setting is elementary, high school, or university. (You may want to refer to the activity "Class Begins" in DeCapua & Wintergerst, 2016, pages 37–38.)

3. Keep a journal or notebook about pragmatic differences.

Now that you have developed an understanding of pragmatic differences and how much language use reflects underlying cultural norms and values, make notes on what you (or your students and/or colleagues) notice when interacting with speakers from other languages and cultures. How is language used differently?

For example, in which contexts do people thank, apologize, or demand? How do they express gratitude or displeasure? What age, gender, generational, and/or status differences are there?

In addition, if journals and blog entries were started in Myth 1 (see What We Can Do), review these entries and consider re-evaluating them in light of the discussion in this chapter on pragmatic differences.

4. Prepare mini-scenarios that illustrate potential areas of pragmatic misunderstandings.

After each mini-scenario (critical incident), offer three or four possible responses, only one of which is appropriate in English. Ask students to read the scenarios, make their choices, and discuss their responses, focusing on cultural norms underlying each response. (See Myth 1, What We Can Do.)

SAMPLE MINI-SCENARIO 1

Diana is sitting at a desk in the classroom as Mervat, a fellow classmate, enters and sits next to her. Diana notices that Mervat is wearing a beautiful scarf so she compliments her on it. Mervat takes off her scarf, hands it to Diana, and tells her it is now hers.

   a. Diana's behavior was inappropriate. People should not compliment each other unless they are family or very close friends.
   b. Mervat should have just thanked Diana.
   c. Mervat's behavior was appropriate. When people compliment something, it means they want it.
   d. Diana should have thanked Mervat, immediately put on the scarf, and should bring her a gift soon.

In another type of mini-scenario or critical incident, a situation is presented that can be interpreted in various ways, as shown here in Sample Mini-Scenario 2.

────────────── SAMPLE MINI-SCENARIO 2

A U.S. teacher is speaking with Mrs. Torres, a parent from Mexico. The teacher says, "It's important that Sonia spend at least an hour doing her math homework every night. Can you please check on her at home to be sure that she does so? Sonia will make so much more progress if she does this." In response, Mrs. Torres says, "I will talk with her."

What do you think Mrs. Torres meant with her response? Why?

There is no one answer to the question posed at the end of the mini-scenario. Some students may suggest that Mrs. Torres' response "I will talk with her" is an affirmative response indicating that she will follow the teacher's suggestion. Other students may argue that Mrs. Torres' response means that she is not really committing to anything specific because her response is vague. Some students might wonder if Mrs. Torres' response is related to her coming from a high-context culture; others whether it might be a language issue.

What this mini-scenario illustrates how it is not always easy to understand what someone means, particularly when we interact with people from different cultures and languages. It is important to clarify meaning by restating, asking again, or summarizing what one thinks has been said. For instance, the U.S. teacher could have followed up with a reformulation and question such as, "Good, then we agree that you will pay attention to be sure that she does her homework, right?"

5. Help to develop students' observation and analytical skills.

Ask students to observe and analyze how speakers are interacting with one another in authentic materials, such as clips from movies or TV shows. Clips showing instances of pragmatic failure, either cross-culturally or between members of a single culture, are particularly useful. Some movies and TV shows that are useful for this activity are: *The Gods Grew Tired of Us, Lost in Translation, My Big Fat Greek Wedding,* and *Spanglish.* Some TV shows are: *Friends, The Office,* or *Mind Your Language.* (More ideas and specific suggestions on how to do this, along with a sample observation template, can be found in DeCapua & Wintergerst, 2016, pages 303–308.).

6. Provide students with scenarios and ask them to role play the situations.

Just as athletes often tape and watch their practice sessions to identify problems and refine their skills, students can learn by watching videos of themselves in different scenarios. Videotape the situations, play them for the students, and then discuss what is said as a class. Remind students that critiquing is not the same as criticizing and that feedback on performance should be practical and encouraging.

Sample Scenario 1 for the Role-Play
Student A has missed a week of class because of illness.
❑ Student A asks the teacher for an extension on the assignment.   ❑ Student A asks Student B for help in catching up on the missed work.

Sample Scenario 2 for the Role-Play
The students are working in pairs. Student A and Student B are engaged in a very loud discussion, which is bothering Students C and D who are sitting next to them.
❑ Student C asks Students A & B to be quieter.   ▪ A few minutes later, they continue their loud discussion.   ❑ Student D complains to Students A & B.   ❑ Student A apologizes.

Everyone knows what a good instructional environment is.

In the Real World . . .

Teachers incorporate the dominant cultural beliefs of a society in which they live. In cultures that highly value hierarchy, authority, and respect for one's elders, teachers are viewed as the repositories and arbiters of knowledge and they are prepared to transmit that knowledge to their students for them to absorb and store. In cultures in which knowledge is regarded as deriving from questioning and exploration, teachers are perceived as facilitators of a learning process in which students take active roles in generating, organizing, and reflecting on this knowledge. Two classrooms and observations follow to illustrate this point.

Teacher A:

The classroom is arranged in rows, with the teacher's desk and a lectern in the front. Students sit quietly in their seats while the students listen to Teacher A. There is no interaction among students or between Teacher A and the students.

Observer 1: It is good to see students so attentive to the teacher's instruction. We can see that they are truly learning from this teacher.

Observer 2: Why isn't the teacher engaging with the students? Why aren't the students asking any questions? How will the students show they are engaged or developing higher-order thinking skills?

Teacher B:

The classroom is arranged in pods, four desks to a pod. The teacher's desk is on one side of the classroom. The noise level is high as students move about the room while working collaboratively on assignments in their different groups and centers. There is constant interaction among the students and between Teacher B and the students.

Observer 1: The teacher lacks control. Why isn't the teacher delivering instruction? How can these students learn much of anything? Students need to listen and learn from the expert.

Observer 2: This is a learner-centered classroom in which students are actively engaged in learning. Their teacher is observing, providing feedback, and conducting ongoing informal assessment. This is what education is about.

The opposing interpretations of the same classrooms clearly indicate the differing concepts of effective teaching and learning. Teacher A represents what we find in many educational systems around the world. Because teachers are the knowledge experts, it is their role to present the material and it is the student's role to learn what is being taught. Students receive knowledge through teacher-delivered instruction with little to no student participation unless specifically called upon by the teacher. And when students are called upon to answer, the questions are usually to check that students have been paying attention and understand the material.

The second teacher, B, reflects the dominant school of thought intrinsic to the U.S. and many Western educational systems—namely, the belief that learning is based on questioning, which comes from the Socratic tradition of ancient Greece: Thoughtful, targeted questioning will direct students to attain knowledge. Even when classrooms are teacher-centered, students are still expected and encouraged to question because learning is regarded as a process of exploring, examining, and evaluating information. As students actively engage in such practices, they learn. It is also exemplified in a well-known quote from Albert Einstein, "The important thing is not to stop questioning." Kuhn (2012) emphasizes the centrality of questioning in *The Structure of Scientific Revolutions* where he lays out how change in knowledge, or a paradigm shift in understanding, only occurs when current beliefs are challenged. We can sum up the belief of the importance of questioning authority—or the current state of knowledge—by the mantra we encounter constantly in all forms of media, "Think outside the box."

Cultural variation in what constitutes learning and teaching are illustrated in the brief scenarios and observer evaluations: What counts as learning? How should instruction be delivered? And, what are the expectations of and assumptions made by both teachers and students? Figure 6.1 visually conceptualizes the difference in these polar opposite viewpoints of teaching.

The Role of the Teacher

Anyone who has ever taught has most likely experienced a class where a carefully prepared lesson or activity fell flat. In diverse classrooms, lessons that don't work can be the result of a mismatch of teacher and learner assumptions about what constitutes good learning. For example, an increasingly popular pedagogical strategy in U.S. classrooms is cooperative learning and small group work, as illustrated by Teacher B's class. This is rooted in the belief that cooperative learning better engages students in their own learning

Figure 6.1: Comparing Linear and Cyclical Learning

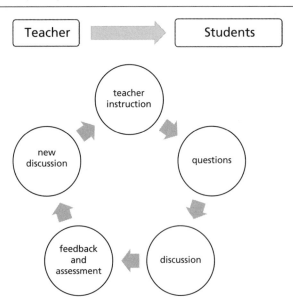

process, provides space for questioning, and increases the likelihood that all students will participate rather than just the more vocal students (Gillies, 2014; Slavin, 2011). Yet from the perspective of other cultures, as was the case for Observer 1 in Teacher B's class, cooperative learning is a waste of time. Teachers are the authorities. It is the teacher's job to deliver the subject matter and it is the students' job to learn. If teachers are not imparting knowledge, why are they in the classroom?

This respect for and belief in the teacher as the authority is also evidenced outside the classroom. My student Sonia shared her experience as the mother of an eight-year-old when she first moved to the U.S.:

We moved to the U.S. when my son was in his fourth year of school. I was shocked at my first parent-teacher conference. The teacher gave both my son and me options and suggestions, and acted like our friend, like the three of us were equals. I didn't know what to do or say. How could I or my son decide? We are not teachers. In my country when we are parents and send our children to school, we entrust our children to their teachers. Teachers are like gods, they know what to teach, how to teach, and deserve our respect and our children's respect. Here I feel it's like the teachers are selling school and learning to students and parents like they are customers.

From Sonia's point of view, she was being thrust into an unfamiliar role, one that went contrary to her experiences and beliefs. The teacher was involving Sonia and her son in a shared evaluation and decision-making process about his learning, rather than assuming the role of expert and sole decision-maker who then informs the parent and son what these decisions are.

The Role of the Student

Some common questions and statements found in U.S. classrooms are:

"What's your opinion about X?"

"It's your decision."

"I don't think I agree with that."

"Can you explain again?"

"I don't understand how this works."

These questions and statements illustrate how discussions, questions, and open dialogue on lesson content are typical. Students are encouraged and expected to be active participants in the learning process, voice their opinions, ask for clarifications, make their own decisions and judgments, and ask teachers for help when they don't understand or know how to proceed. This, however, does not hold true across cultures. As this quote from Mai, a student from Thailand, illustrates, students from other cultures may feel very differently about classroom interactions:

> When I first came here, it seemed the American students were always asking questions. Speaking up—just even thinking about it—terrified me. They were so confident and comfortable, and they shared their opinions so freely, even contradicting teachers. I felt so uncomfortable and embarrassed and thought why do teachers allow this behavior? Even now I sometimes feel the same way.

Students from cultures that promote respect for authority and discourage outward displays of strong feelings and emotions are generally uncomfortable participating in class discussions and questioning teachers' actions, knowledge, or information. In their cultural concept of the role of learners, students from any culture with controlled teacher-centered learning settings do not feel qualified to evaluate critically the perspectives, judgments, or conclusions of experts (Fidalgo-Neto et al., 2009; Pai, Adler, & Shadlow, 2006).

In cultures that have been influenced by Confucianism (e.g., China and Korea), students are expected to be obedient and respectful to authority figures, which includes teachers. Students educated in such educational systems find the questions introducing this section difficult and even stressful because teachers are the knowledgeable authorities, the experts, the "fonts of knowledge." Likewise, challenging the teacher, asking for explanations, or indicating confusion are regarded as having the potential to disrupt harmony and threaten face: How can students, who are the learners, challenge the knowledge of experts? Does my question imply the teacher didn't do a good job of presenting the material? What if the teacher doesn't know the answer? What if students ask stupid questions and embarrass themselves in front of their classmates?

What the Research Says . . .

The chapter began by mentioning how teachers' pedagogical practices reflect and promote the cultural norms, values, and beliefs of a culture. As we saw in the discussion of Teacher B's class and cooperative learning (In the Real World), what are considered "best practices" in the U.S. are not universally applicable (Watkins, 2000). Students from other cultures with different values and beliefs about teaching may find U.S. pedagogical practices—such as the notion of teachers as facilitators of learning and collaborative learning in general—frustrating and bewildering (Bista, 2012; Smith & Hu, 2013). In China, and other Confucian-influenced East Asian cultures, for example, the prevailing pedagogy today, and for hundreds of years, has emphasized systematized, teacher-centered, direct instructional delivery as a means of promoting the collective good. A robust regard for the authority of the teacher is also evident in Latin American cultures in which a core value is *respeto*, or respect or obedience to parents, elders, and authority figures (Marín & VanOss Marín, 1991). Many other cultures globally, whether Sudanese, Afghani, or Indian, have similar perspectives (Flaitz, 2006).

Underlying the cooperative learning approach is the broader constructivist philosophy underpinning education in the U.S. that views learning as the construction of knowledge (Joyce, Weil, & Calhoun, 2014). To construct knowledge, learners engage in an active interplay between knowledge, experience, and ideas. Knowledge is not merely transmitted to learners, but the learners themselves actively participate in the learning process by participating in experiences that require them to react, integrate, and reorganize information, or in other words, *question*. It is through this process that new knowledge and new paradigms come to be created (see, e.g., Bruner, 1966; Dewey, 1916; Vygotsky, 1978).

This constructivist philosophy of education aligns with European notions of critical and analytical thinking that are by no means the norm worldwide (Dahl, 2010). In many cultures, rote learning prevails as the primary approach. Rote learning is generally characterized as the memorization and recall of information with minimal or no application, investigation, or exploration. Arab cultures tend to rely heavily on this type of learning as it aligns with common pedagogical practices for teaching children religious scripture (Etri, 2014). Rote learning is also the norm in sub-Saharan Africa (Altinyelken, 2012; Hardman, Abd-Kadir, & Smith, 2008), in much of Latin America (Flaitz, 2006), and in Asia (Chang et al., 2011; Zulfikar, 2013). Although it has been argued that not all rote learning is identical (Kember & Watkins, 2010), there are genuinely divergent beliefs underlying rote learning versus constructivist learning.

Despite calls for and attempts at change, the adoption and implementation of more learner-centered pedagogy remains slow or is found primarily in privileged schools, much of this due to profoundly embedded differences in cultural values regarding teaching and learning (Gitsaki, 2011; McGuire, 2007; Ngware, Mutisya, & Oketch, 2012). In countries strongly influenced by Confucianism, for instance, much of the failure to change traditional pedagogical practices has been attributed to deep-seated Confucian beliefs about obedience to authority and respect for one's elders (McNaught, 2012; Yin, Lee, & Wang, 2014).

Thus, since questioning, exploring, offering opinions, and disagreeing are not part of non-constructivist learning traditions, students from such educational systems often have difficulties adjusting to, and may challenge the effectiveness of, U.S. classrooms and pedagogical practices.

Collectivism and Individualism in the Classroom

As discussed in Myth 2, collectivism and individualism are essential cultural concepts. The influence of these two concepts plays a significant role in educational practices and beliefs. At times students from collectivistic cultures behave collectively in learning situations but appear to behave individually at other times. The underlying motivations or reasons for these seemingly contradictory behaviors still align with their collectivistic cultural orientation.

Let's start with competition. Academic competitiveness in school exists in most cultures, whether collectivistic or individualistic. In many cultures, school systems are based on national exams designed to allow only the best students—or at least the best test-takers—to succeed. Schools encourage competition, contests, and intellectual rivalry as preparation and training for the rigorous examination system (Behera & Pramanik, 2012). In more collectivistic cultures, students' desire to compete and succeed is extrinsic and communal. They strive to perform well because how well they do reflects on their group as a whole (Hofstede, 1986). What one person accomplishes promotes success for everyone, making the family proud and/or being able to better support the extended family.

For students in more individualistic cultures, on the other hand, the desire to compete and succeed is intrinsic and personal (King, McInerney, & Watkins, 2012). They are motivated primarily to be the best for personal reward or benefit or to earn praise from the teacher so they that can get into the university of their choice. Accomplishments represent the achievements and success of the individual.

Motivation is an important factor in learning. However, there are significant cultural differences in understanding where motivation comes from, or in other words, how to motivate students. Li

(2012), in her extensive exploration of the differences in learning between the East and West, particularly U.S. and Chinese students, argues that a key difference lies in how motivation is regarded. In the U.S. (and other Western cultures), motivation is regarded as largely intrinsic—that is, coming from within the learner. Therefore, educators emphasize processes to stimulate motivation in each individual student. If something is enjoyable, interesting, and stimulating, students will want to learn. For East Asians coming from the collectivistic Confucian tradition, on the other hand, such factors are not as important as others. In the Confucian tradition, learning is perceived as extrinsically motivated and undertaken to cultivate one's self. Learning requires students to not only learn academic knowledge but to also develop morally and socially so that they can contribute meaningfully to the group or society. Extrinsic family and group goals (collectivistic goals, that is), rather than personal goals, are frequently motivators for students to do well.

Let's consider cooperative learning through the lens of collectivism. Chinese students, although members of a highly collectivist culture, often have difficulties (at least initially) with cooperative learning practices and expectations in U.S. classrooms (Huang & Brown, 2009). Given their collectivistic orientation, one would expect Chinese students to adapt readily to cooperative learning; yet, since their prior learning experiences have taken place for the most part, if not entirely, in highly structured, authoritarian classrooms, they are not comfortable with or prepared for cooperative learning classrooms when they first encounter them. The less-structured environment, the amount of individual class participation, and the different expectations about learning are jarring (Cheng, 2012). This contrasts to the tendency of Chinese students to quickly form informal learning groups outside the classroom, a manifestation of their collectivistic orientation (Ibarra, 2001).

Mexican students, who are also members of a collectivistic culture, frequently have fewer difficulties when they encounter cooperative learning in U.S. schools. This is because they tend to be comfortable with being active participants in classroom settings, especially if language is not a barrier. From the U.S. perspective, Mexican classrooms tend to be stricter and more formal, yet a great deal of student talk and interaction is common. Even when the teacher is talking, students will discuss class content and interject comments and questions (Jiménez, Smith, & Martínez-León, 2003). However, depending on which school in Mexico that students come from, there will be differences in how comfortable they are with cooperative learning and with less structured and less formal, teacher-student interaction (de Souza, 2013; Andrews, 2016).

While keeping in mind the danger of overgeneralizing Latinos as a single ethnic group, the overall Latino sense of collectivism extends to helping others and attending to their needs, even to those who are of medium closeness, like friends or classmates (Arevalo, So, & McNaughton-Cassill, 2016). There is an implicit commitment to aid others and students will spontaneously help their classmates understand material and complete assignments during class time, placing less emphasis on competing against each other academically because learning is regarded as a shared or group responsibility (Rothstein-Fisch & Trumbull, 2008). For U.S. teachers, however, there is a fine line between helping another student and sharing too much information. The latter is regarded as copying, is heavily frowned upon, and is considered cheating.

Plagiarism

While at times sharing information in the U.S. may be regarded as helping, appropriating someone else's work as one's own is always regarded as plagiarism. *Plagiarism* is a highly negative concept. In individualistic cultures such as the U.S., ideas, concepts, and words are considered to belong to the individual who first suggested or conceptualized them and are regarded as being "owned" by that

- Can't over analyze that chinese, Mexicans will be comfortable in cooperative learning.
- highly structured / authoritarian cultures - chinese

person. When another person wishes to use any of these words or ideas, whether in written or oral form, it is necessary to cite the author or creator. Failure to do so is regarded as a form of misrepresentation, or even stealing.

From the collectivist standpoint, intellectual property is a contribution that should be shared. Borrowing any or all of it, even verbatim, is generally more acceptable than in the U.S. Such borrowing or appropriation is a sign of respect for the expertise of the originator or creator of the idea, concept, or words (Hall, 2006; Mundava & Chaudhuri, 2007). Moreover, when students come from educational systems in which the teacher and the text are the authorities, they have not necessarily learned "to put things in their own words." There is the sense that it is best to use what experts have said since they said it so well. Kenneth, a university lecturer in Taiwan explains:

> There is an old Chinese saying, "All written words are copied from the words of others (*tian xia wen zhang yi da chao*)." Basically, this means that you start learning things by copying or imitating. East Asian cultures worship old sayings and proverbs as well as the words of famous individuals; therefore, people tend to use these in their writing. This is also embedded in the education. Most teachers would say something like, "You are nobody and nobody cares about what you say. You need to start your writing with some famous sayings or proverbs." So, using others' words is generally not considered a totally bad thing, although I still think there is a fine line between copying directly and writing something very similar.

When it comes to plagiarism, it is important not to stereotype. Not all students from a collectivistic culture are more likely to plagiarize than students from an individualistic culture. A famous example of plagiarism outside the U.S and in another individualistic culture occurred in Germany in 2011 and again in 2015.

The then-German defense ministers were forced to resign after it was discovered that they had plagiarized significant portions of their doctoral dissertations. It should also be noted that plagiarism issues are not limited to international students. Plagiarism across disciplines, regardless of language and culture among U.S. university students, is a major problem (Doss et al., 2016).

Yet, plagiarism itself is not easy to define precisely. As Mott-Smith, Tomaš, and Kostka (2017) point out, even among U.S. university professors, there is not 100 percent agreement of what plagiarism is, beyond instances of a person intentionally copying verbatim large portions of text without proper attribution, as in the case of the German defense ministers. What exactly constitutes plagiarism is even more bewildering for international students, particularly when their prior school experiences conflict with their teachers' interpretation of plagiarism, as reflected in Kenneth's quote. Furthermore, as Mott-Smith, Tomaš, and Kostka (2017) note, the term *plagiarism* itself refers to a broad range of practices, some of which are intentionally deceitful, such as hiring someone else to write a paper or purposefully lifting large portions of text. On the other hand, particularly for language learners, there are other types of what may be regarded as unintentional plagiarism, such as not having a strong command of English or lacking the ability to paraphrase or cite accurately because they have not learned how to do so. (See Mott-Smith, Tomaš, & Kostka, 2017, for a comprehensive examination of issues surrounding plagiarism and sample lessons.)

Class Participation

Active class participation is the norm in U.S. classrooms, and in many classes points are awarded for such participation. Students from other cultures may feel uncomfortable participating, regardless of their language proficiency. Even those who are proficient in English may not engage in class discussions because of different conversational norms governing pause lengths, interruptions, and overlaps (see Myth 3). If students don't know how to break into a conversation or retain the floor when they are the one speaking, they are not going to participate much (Nakane, 2005).

Even conventional teacher-centered classrooms in the U.S. expect students to participate. Particularly common are teacher-student question-answer exchanges known as IRF—initiation, response, feedback (Cazden, 2001), which basically work like this:

- The teacher asks a question. (initiation)
- Students raise their hands (or indicate with their eyes).
- The teacher calls on a student.
- The student answers the question while the rest of the class listens. (response)
- The teacher offers feedback on the student's response. (feedback)

Students from other cultures may not be accustomed to this type of teacher-student interaction. Some of this may be due to prior educational experiences in systems that reward listening while discouraging any type of participation (Tatar, 2005). Or, students may come from educational systems in which teachers criticize, ridicule, or punish students for giving wrong responses, making students reluctant to respond to questions (Agbenyega & Deku, 2011). Students from more collectivistic cultures may feel awkward about being singled out and put in the spotlight, regardless of whether or not they are otherwise outgoing or have strong language proficiency.

Student identity and face are other factors in student reluctance to participate. Non-native speakers may purposely choose not to participate actively because they find themselves in classrooms in which teaching practices don't match their own expectations and beliefs about their identity as a learner, or how they feel they learn best and how they should act as students (Norton, 2001). Moreover, students who strongly identify themselves as members of their home culture and feel like cultural outsiders with different communication styles, regardless of language proficiency, may be reluctant to adopt the active role of a U.S. student (Zheng, 2010).

Anxiety and stress also play a role (Gu, Schweisfurth, & Day, 2009), making classroom participation less likely. Students who are attending school in a new culture with different cultural norms and expectations frequently experience culture shock. This is the distress people feel when they are placed in an environment in which familiar routines, conversational patterns, and behaviors are no longer operative (DeCapua & Wintergerst, 2016; Oberg, 1960). Experiencing culture shock causes anxiety and stress; anxious and stressed students are less likely to participate in class (Ward, Bochner, & Furnham, 2005).

Two other factors that may affect student participation are culturally specific background knowledge and gender concerns. When topics are context-embedded, non-U.S. students may not have the background to participate in discussions. Historical events, literary references, and cultural icons in sports, music, TV, or politics may be unfamiliar. Female students, especially those from Muslim cultures, may feel uncomfortable or unable to participate freely in the presence of male students (Brisk, 2011).

And finally, wait (pause) time after asking a question and teacher expectation are also factors (see Myth 3). In many cultures, speakers take time to reflect after they have been asked a question. This indicates that one is taking the time to consider one's response carefully; responding too quickly indicates a lack of thought (Bista, 2012). U.S. teachers who are accustomed to shorter wait times when engaging in IRF or other question-answer routines may inadvertently interrupt the reflection and thought processes of their students by not allowing them enough response time.

In sum, teachers of culturally and linguistically diverse students will often find that these students do not meet their expectations or share their beliefs about what a good student is. This is often the result of a mismatch between culturally based beliefs about teaching and learning between the teacher and the students.

Giving Feedback

In examining cultural differences in the roles of teachers and students, we need to look at another common activity in the learning cycle: providing feedback to the learner. We find that, as with other aspects of classroom interaction, cultural beliefs about the role of teacher feedback influence the type and purpose of feedback:

- Should teacher feedback focus on students' shortcomings so that they will try harder?
- Should teacher feedback emphasize the positive so that students feel empowered and encouraged?
- Or, should teacher feedback be a combination of the two?

In answering these questions, it's important to take into consideration underlying beliefs about teaching and learning.

Like so much of what we have discussed in the different chapters, what constitutes appropriate feedback varies across cultures. In France and China, teacher feedback includes more criticism than what is considered appropriate in the U.S. because there is a different perspective on the purpose of feedback. In France and China, along with many other countries, there is the belief that feedback that focuses on students' mistakes allows them to recognize where they need to improve, whereas praise leads to overconfidence (Santagata, 2004; Tangie, 2015).

My student Bonnie, an American married to a Frenchman and living in France, describes her experience with her daughter's teachers in this way:

> French teachers think nothing of bluntly pointing out a student's mistakes and giving very little praise. It was shocking to me at first because I was used to American teachers who praised effort and who were more focused on encouraging students through positive feedback. My daughter, and it seems everyone else here in France, is fine with how it's done here because it's what they're used to. And now that I've gotten used to it, I wonder if the French way gives less a sense of entitlement to kids in school.

Similarly, Qin (2014) quotes Ashley, an American studying in China:

> Today my Chinese teacher told me "you are not creative at all" in front of the whole class. This made me very mad. I argued back, "So who do you think is creative in our class?" The teacher pointed to another student and said, "He, he is more creative than you and you should learn from him." I felt as if he was trying to humiliate me in class. I cannot understand how he could say that as a teacher. In some cases, that behavior might even get him into trouble with the administration if he was teaching in an American public high school. (p. 73)

In the U.S., educators believe that supportive feedback builds and maintains students' self-confidence, motivates learners, and makes them become better learners (Fong & Yuen, 2016). When giving feedback that includes criticism, teachers generally "sandwich" the criticism (Dohrenwend, 2002; Just, 2007). In other words, they lead in with something positive (top of the bun), give the criticism (the meat), and end with another positive statement (bottom of the bun). In this way, teachers mitigate the criticism and encourage student confidence. Students coming from an educational background where criticism as feedback is common may find themselves confused by this "hamburger" or "sandwich" model of feedback and find it insincere or unhelpful.

Closely related to feedback is praise. U.S. teachers often praise students as an appropriate strategy for recognizing the efforts and accomplishments of individuals. It is part of what is considered good feedback and it spotlights the individual. For Asian and sub-Saharan African students, teacher praise can be uncomfortable and embarrassing. Modesty and being an inconspicuous member of a group are highly valued, while singling out one individual for recognition is frowned upon (Nhung, 2014; Ruxin, 2013).

U.S. parents also react positively to praise about their children from teachers (Reinke, Lewis-Palmer, & Martin, 2007). Parents from cultures that do not encourage open praise react differently to praise from their children's teachers. They typically downplay the praise by contradicting or downplaying with responses such as, "My child isn't as good as Mrs. ___'s son" or "My child can do better when he tries harder" (DeCapua & Wintergerst, 2016). U.S. teachers unfamiliar with these types of responses are likely to be surprised and perhaps wonder why the parents aren't supportive of their children and their achievements.

In addition to such factors as modesty, humility, and blending in with the group, different cultures have varying interpretations of achievement. In the U.S., as in most Western cultures, achievement is viewed as the result of innate ability, intelligence, and hard work that develops "natural" abilities (assuming equal socioeconomic circumstances and opportunities). I was not a particularly graceful child, did not do well in ballet classes, and quickly dropped out. From the U.S. point of view, why continue with something I had no talent for and was not finding pleasure in? Motivation comes from success and since I was not having success, I was not motivated to continue.

From the East Asian perspective, the problem with my failure at ballet was that I didn't try hard enough. Had I stuck with ballet classes for several years and practiced intensely, I would have most certainly improved and enjoyed it once I was able to succeed to at least some degree. Innate ability and intelligence are secondary to hard work (Li, 2012). Only when you have worked very hard at something do you know whether you can do it well and whether you enjoy it. We see this perspective reflected in the earlier parental response to the teacher's praise of a student, "My child can do better when he tries harder." Students are exhorted by their parents to strive harder because only if they have tried as hard as possible will they know what they are truly capable of achieving. Motivation comes from believing that perseverance and diligence lead to eventual success (Huang, 2014).

What We Can Do . . .

1. Offer students opportunities to practice participation in the classroom by scaffolding with sentence starters.

Sentence starters are phrases to help students practice engaging in and managing communicative interactions. They not only scaffold discussions, but also allow teachers to introduce and practice polite ways (from the U.S. perspective) of conversation.

Sample	
Purpose	**Starter**
Add to what the speaker has said	*I would like to add that . . . .* *I agree with what _____ said because . . . .* *We can also think of it this way . . . .*
Take a stance	*But if we look at the data / what the author says, I think that. . . .* *The reason I feel / believe that . . . .* *Another way to think about this is . . . .*
Hold (prevent someone from taking) the floor	*Please let me finish . . . .* *One moment please . . . .* *That's a great thought/idea/suggestion, but I'd like to finish my . . . .*

2. Use mini-scenarios (critical incidents).

Mini-scenarios can be used to explore cultural clashes related to the classroom that stem from the different cultural factors discussed in this chapter. (See Myth 1, What We Can Do.)

SAMPLE MINI SCENARIO 1

A group of parents of students who recently arrived from various countries in southeast Asia come to the principal's office to complain:

"Our children do not get enough homework."

"There are too many activities and games during class time. The teachers must lecture more."

"There are students who talk so much that our children can't learn from the teacher."

1. What cultural factors might underlie the parents' concerns?
2. How might you, either as a teacher or administrator, address such concerns?

SAMPLE MINI SCENARIO 2

Several colleagues are discussing some of their international students:

"They never raise their hands when I ask questions."

"They never present or defend their views in class."

"They keep asking me what elective courses they should take, rather than deciding what they want."

"They always grumble when I have them do group work."

1. What cultural factors might underlie the students' behaviors on one hand and the teachers' criticisms on the other?
2. What suggestions might you offer the teachers, based on what you have learned in this chapter and/or your personal experience?

3. Do not equate silence with disengagement or disinterest.

Students may be participating by other means such as active listening, note-taking, thinking about, or reflecting on the material. Find ways other than oral responses to give them opportunities to share what they have learned. In addition, provide opportunities for small group or partner discussions and activities. Such discussions and activities encourage students who may be uncomfortable with whole class discussion to participate. Ask one person in each group to report back to the whole class with a summary of their discussion and findings. Alternate the students who are responsible for reporting to the whole class.

4. Show your students samples of what plagiarism is.

All students may not share the same understanding of what constitutes plagiarism. To ensure that they understand what you consider plagiarism:

- Review exactly what you consider constitutes plagiarism at your institution.
- Provide specific examples of unintentional plagiarism for class discussion and analysis, demonstrate what students need to do to avoid such plagiarism, and practice these strategies with them.
- Avoid reacting punitively when students produce evidence of unintentional plagiarism. Instead work with them on why this is plagiarism, so that they can learn strategies for avoiding such behaviors.

Ready-made lessons for helping students understand plagiarism are available in *Teaching Effective Source Use* (Mott-Smith, Tomaš, & Kostka, 2017).

5. Learn about different parenting styles.

Pre-service and in-service teachers will benefit from viewing and reading about various cultural values, parenting styles, and expectations and from considering how they might reflect views on teaching and learning. For example, the documentary *Babies*, by the French director Thomas Balmès, follows four children from birth through their first year in four culturally different countries, Namibia, Japan, Mongolia, and the U.S. The documentary is set to music with no words and leaves it up to viewers to draw their own conclusions from the spontaneous, natural scenes. This also gives viewers valuable insights into culturally diverse parenting styles.

Battle Hymn of the Tiger Mom, written by Amy Chua, a Chinese-American, describes how she raised her American-born children in very strict, traditional Chinese ways. The book elicited a great deal of debate, much of which can easily be found on the internet.

7

By the time students get to middle or high school, they know how to be a student.

In the Real World . . .

Mr. Bisserby had fifteen years of experience in a high school, teaching all levels of ESL and ninth grade English Language Arts (ELA). When his town began receiving large numbers of language learners with limited prior schooling, his district decided to start a newcomer program designed for these students. Mr. Bisserby immediately volunteered to teach in this program. Mr. Bisserby is a hard-working, caring, and dedicated teacher who very much wants his students to succeed. One of his classes is a beginner newcomer ESL/ELA class with thirteen students from seven different countries speaking six different languages and three different dialects of one language. Let's look at Mr. Bisserby's class, nine weeks after the beginning of the term.

Last week each student was given a photocopy of a short, adapted ESL text of a Chinese folktale with black and white illustrations. They had started reading this tale together in the previous class. For homework, the students were to write three short sentences about the story using vocabulary from that lesson. On the homework worksheet, Mr. Bisserby had listed the vocabulary and provided some sentence starters to help them write their sentences, such as *The dragon* ____ and *Shen is* ____.

Mr. Bisserby began today's lesson by projecting the folktale on a screen, summarizing it, and then reading the entire tale aloud. After this, the students followed along as he re-read the story slowly; he underlined key words on the projected copy and explained them. He stopped periodically to ask questions about what he had just read to check their comprehension. Next, Mr. Bisserby called on different students to read sentences out loud. Then, he put students into pairs, told them to alternate reading the first two short paragraphs to each other, underline the same words on their copy that he had underlined, and write definitions for those words. Near the end of the period, the students shared their homework answers with each other and checked them. For this night's homework, Mr. Bisserby gave the students a worksheet for practicing the new vocabulary words and writing three more sentences using the vocabulary.

There were many reasons why one might expect this lesson to be successful for this population of students. Folktales, fables, and legends are a popular and common genre across cultures, and Mr. Bisserby believed that all students would find something familiar in the lesson. He chose a folktale from China since many of his students were from Asia, and he thought some of them might even know this one. The students had opportunities to support and learn from each other as they worked in pairs (and one group of three). Mr. Bisserby tried to ensure that everyone was attentive and participating, both during the teacher-directed portion of the lesson and during the pair work. Nevertheless, despite the many factors indicating that the lesson would be an effective one, it missed the mark.

In observing the lesson, I noticed a number of times where there was a disconnect between the teacher and his students. Here are a few of the things I noticed:

- When Mr. Bisserby stopped to ask questions during his reading of the text, only two students responded.
- When Mr. Bisserby tried to help the students understand a question by pointing to one of the black and white illustrations, only the same two students responded.
- At one point, Mr. Bisserby asked one of these two students to translate his question to another student sitting next to her after he asked him a question and he didn't respond. She did, but even then the student was still not able to respond in his native language.
- Of the thirteen students, only the same two who had responded to Mr. Bisserby's questions were able to read the sentences aloud when he called on them. Another three students read some of their assigned sentences, but they randomly called out words, usually ones that started with the same letter, such as saying *day* instead of reading *door.*
- Eight of the students had difficulty matching the underlined words on the projected text to their photocopied text. Mr. Bisserby had to go to each pair and physically demonstrate how to find the words on the projected text, underline them on their copies, and copy the definition.
- Several times Mr. Bisserby had to remind students to write on the lines in their notebooks and on the homework worksheet.

During our debriefing session, Mr. Bisserby expressed his feelings about this lesson and about teaching this group of students in general:

> No matter how slow I go, no matter how I break down the material, they aren't progressing like my other language learners. I'm giving them lots of extra support, but it doesn't seem to help.

Mr. Bisserby's difficulty was due to the fact that he was making several critical assumptions about instruction, all of them based on his own culturally influenced prior learning and teaching experiences. These assumptions, for example, included that his adolescent students would have basic literacy skills and would understand how to work with text to extract meaning.

The students in Mr. Bisserby's class are unlike most other language learners who come to U.S. schools and have had age-appropriate formal education. The primary need of these language learners is to learn English and to catch up on content knowledge specific to their new country, such as U.S. history. Pedagogy, texts, and materials for language learners after kindergarten or the early primary grades assume foundational literacy skills and are geared to the "typical" learner. However, the students in Mr. Bisserby's class had significantly different prior learning experiences that took place in out-of-school contexts.

Language learners like those in Mr. Bisserby's newcomer class are often referred to as *SLIFE (students with limited or interrupted formal education)* to distinguish them from other language learners (DeCapua, Smathers, & Tang, 2009). These students, unlike other language learners, do not have age-appropriate literacy skills, content-knowledge, and academic ways of thinking and understanding the world. Because their culturally influenced prior learning experiences have taken place primarily outside formal classrooms and literacy has not been central in their lives, their prior learning experiences do not align with Mr. Bisserby's assumptions and expectations about learning and teaching.

SLIFE (a plural term—students) do not have the same background in formal education as other language learners for a number of reasons. For SLIFE who have had some schooling, it may have been *limited* because:

- they may have had to travel long distances to school particularly if they come from a rural area, making it difficult to attend when the weather was bad.
- schools were open irregularly and/or teachers were often absent.
- they may have attended schools that did not provide sufficient grade-level content-area knowledge, frequently the result of a lack of trained teachers and adequate learning resources.
- the focus in teaching may have been on teacher lectures, rote learning, and verbatim dictation and recall.
- class sizes may been large, with forty or more students.
- schools may have charged fees and/or students may have been required to purchase uniforms, school supplies, such as pencils, pens, notebooks, and even textbooks—expenses that many families may not have been able to afford for more than a few years.

For other SLIFE, their schooling may have been *interrupted*— that is, they may have been forced to miss school for at least two to three years—because:

- there was war, civil unrest, or a natural disaster such as an earthquake.
- they needed to work either at home or outside to help the family.
- they migrated, moving from place to place (or country) over a series of months and/or years.

These are among the many factors that describe the educational experiences of these students and provide a sense of who they are.

Because of limited, interrupted, and in some cases, no prior formal education, the needs of these students are different from those who have had age-appropriate formal education: They have low or no literacy, and those who do have some literacy generally have only basic decoding skills. Others, even if their literacy is in a non-alphabetic language, can transfer literacy skills to the new language.

SLIFE are also missing the content knowledge of their peers, both peers in their home country and in the U.S. While other English learners may need to learn content specific to their new country, they have the underlying foundations of subject matter, unlike SLIFE who may not have learned even basic content. Simply put, SLIFE have not had opportunities to develop identities as learners within the framework of formal education and its inherent assumptions and expectations. They do not understand school routines and behaviors, academic ways of thinking, or how to be a learner. The differences between the two groups is summarized in Figure 7.1.

Let's return to Mr. Bisserby's class and his feelings and think about both in terms of what you now know about this population of students. Notice the disconnect between what he expected and wanted and what the students could and did do. What is happen-

Figure 7.1: SLIFE and Non-SLIFE Language Learners

SLIFE	Non-SLIFE
No, interrupted, or limited formal education	Appropriate age-level formal education
Low or no literacy	Age-appropriate literacy in L1
Missing foundational content knowledge	Content knowledge (with cultural differences, e.g., Mexican history instead of U.S. history)
Unfamiliar with "doing school"	Identity as a learner

ing is an example of the human tendency to evaluate others from one's own cultural perspective. In this case, the culture is that of formal education. We may not initially think of schooling as a "culture." This is partly because we are, for the most part, initiated into it at a very young age and it is virtually universal in our national consciousness. We teach from within our own culture of formal education and expect students to be able to engage in basic school practices and think in school-based ways by the time they are in middle and high school. These assumptions are based on our educational experiences and beliefs about teaching and learning in what is commonly referred to as Western-style formal education (Givvin et al., 2005).

For example, Mr. Bisserby expected his SLIFE to be able to work with the written word, despite the fact that they were low-literate learners. He did not have literacy training and therefore did not realize the steps necessary to develop and practice foundational literacy skills. This is illustrated again in Mr. Bisserby's attempt to ask the students to use the drawing to help them understand the story. SLIFE are not comfortable with or used to the two-dimensional world of drawings or diagrams, which incorporate a shared code. Let's explore this further by looking at this illustration. What is it depicting?

Some readers will easily understand that this drawing represents a very thirsty man because they know the code—oval shapes falling down his face means sweat; the three circles indicate his thoughts, etc. However, we cannot assume that SLIFE share the same code given their different learning experiences and low literacy. Mr. Bisserby, while using a common educational scaffold, was not in fact using a scaffold that was meaningful and relevant to his students. The SLIFE were not associating the two-dimensional representational drawings in their reading with concrete objects and figures of the real world.

To understand and meet the needs of SLIFE, we must carefully examine our own assumptions and expectations within the culture of formal education. Without realizing the significantly different learning paradigm of SLIFE, we are likely to confuse cognitive differences with academic deficiencies (Kincheloe, 2006). This leads to a *deficit* view of SLIFE rather than a recognition of *difference* (DeCapua, 2016).

What the Research Says . . .

Learners who come to the U.S. with appropriate grade-level education have a shorter journey in their education than do SLIFE. All learners have to learn a new language and adapt to U.S. ways of teaching and learning, but SLIFE face additional and even greater obstacles. Other language learners are often already literate in their own language, know how to learn in a formal systematic manner, and understand the culture of schooling. They understand what it means to be in a formal classroom, have formed identities as learners in the context of formal education, and can engage in academic ways of thinking. SLIFE, in contrast, in addition to learning English, must also develop literacy skills, acquire missing content knowledge, and learn to engage in school-based tasks based on academic ways of thinking (DeCapua & Marshall, 2011; DeCapua, Smathers, & Tang, 2009). Moreover, SLIFE have not formed identities as learners, or at least not to the degree to be successful in U.S. classrooms.

Informal Ways of Learning

Informal ways of learning refers to learning that takes place in out-of-school contexts and describes the learning experiences familiar to the majority of SLIFE. It is a type of learning that occurs within the context of sociocultural practices and supports individuals in becoming contributing members of their family and community (Gauvain, Beebe, & Zhao, 2011; Rogoff, 2003). Children become competent in what they, their family, and their community need them to learn as they engage in concrete, pragmatic activities. For example, children master cooking, farming, herding, carpentry, selling, trading, and other such skills through mentoring and apprenticeship, and not in school (DeCapua, 2016). This is learning that is not age-based, but rather begins when children feel they are ready or the family or community believes they are ready (Paradise & Rogoff, 2009). There is no formal classroom instruction and literacy is not necessary. What they learn is immediately relevant in their daily lives.

Formal Western-Style Education and Academic Ways of Thinking

Formal Western-style education, on the other hand, is a type of education that is premised on certain fundamental characteristics: literacy, scientific ways of ordering and interpreting the world, formal pedagogical practices, age cohorts for learning, set curriculum, and highly trained teachers. Western-style formal education does not denote education only found in the West, such as in Europe or the Americas. It refers to a type of education that is based on the centrality of literacy and scientific modes of thinking—that is, academic ways of thinking that underlie all aspects of knowledge (Cole, 2005). This Western-style formal education is found globally, with cultural and institutional variations (Grigorenko, 2007).

Let's take two examples to better understand what academic ways of thinking means. Try answering this question:

What do dogs and rabbits have in common?

Readers will easily come up with fur, ears, four legs, and some may even respond with mammals. These responses illustrate an understanding of an abstract system of classification based on specific, identifiable, and shared characteristics (Flynn, 2007). Children raised by parents with formal education are frequently exposed to this way of thinking at an early age through various ways. For example, they may play with educational toys (put the blue block in the square hole), watch videos (*Sesame Street*) and learn songs ("One of These Things Is Not Like the Other") that teach them from an early age the rudiments of classification.

If this same dog and rabbit question is posed to SLIFE, on the other hand, they are more likely to come up with responses such as "You use a dog to hunt rabbits." This answer isn't wrong per se, but it does not meet the requirements understood in the academic way of thinking of defining. The SLIFE response is a pragmatic one, derived from their concrete experience in the real world. Some of you may even have thought of this same answer, but, when given the "correct" or school answer, you understand the logic of "identifiable characteristics."

The question *What do dogs and rabbits have in common* is an example of a variation of the most commonly asked question in Western-style formal classrooms worldwide: *What is ___ ?* as in *What is a tree?* or *What is an owl pellet* (Cazden, 2001; Marshall & DeCapua, 2013). These kinds of questions are known as *definition questions*. The task, defining, entails an academic way of thinking: classification. This academic way of thinking requires identifying distinguishing properties or abstract characteristics, as we did with the dogs and rabbits.

Academic ways of thinking derive from a scientific way of under-standing the world but are not limited to science knowledge. Let's look at this ELA example, *What makes this a fictional piece of writing?* The response entails understanding the academic way of thinking of defining. It requires assigning *fiction* to the broad category of writ-ing, and identifying specific properties or characteristics, namely a description of imaginary events and people that distinguish fiction from other types of writing such as biographies or reports.

Ways of Learning Continuum

We can think of ways of learning as a continuum. On one end are students whose prior learning experiences have been through primarily oral means and the informal ways of learning described earlier. On the other end, we have educators and others who have fully participated in formal education and have strong literacy skills (see Figure 7.2). SLIFE range somewhere along this continuum, depending on how much they have participated in formal educa-tion) but are always closer to the left end (Marshall & DeCapua, 2013).

Regardless of where SLIFE fall along the left end of the contin-uum, we must remember that they come to our formal classrooms with a great deal of prior knowledge and rich experiences, or "funds of knowledge" (González, Moll, & Amanti, 2005). Although these have not been traditionally valued in formal education, effective instruction entails incorporating and honoring what SLIFE bring into our classrooms as we work with them in their transition to the demands, expectations, and requirements of formal education (Bigelow, 2010; DeCapua & Marshall, 2015; Hos, 2014).

Figure 7.2: Ways of Learning Continuum

Informal ways of learning
Oral transmission

Formal education
Literacy

Understanding SLIFE

What happens when SLIFE enter U.S. schools and are placed in age-appropriate grade-level classes, especially at the secondary level? Remember that SLIFE come with prior learning experiences and ways of conceptualizing the world around them that are significantly different from those of U.S. teachers, administrators, staff, and policy-makers. To avoid a deficit view of SLIFE, we need to understand how these prior learning experiences and ways of thinking differ from ours, derived from the distinct culture of formal education.

For many years, I have been conducting teacher training for those working with SLIFE. There are common themes that arise repeatedly as educators struggle to address the needs of this very different population of learners as they encounter school culture. Here we explore some of these themes.

Theme 1: The Basics of School

> Teacher: *How can I even begin to teach these students when they don't know the very basics like where to write their name on their paper, how to write on a line in their notebooks, or even how to open a book?*

For educators, literacy skills are the norm by the time students reach secondary school. Any deviations, especially to the extent of not knowing where to put your name on a paper or not writing on the line, are regarded as a deficit. There is typically little understanding of how a person could reach this age and not know these most basic of tasks. What we need to realize and keep reminding ourselves and our colleagues of is that SLIFE have had significantly different learning experiences and have developed different skills and knowledge including, for instance, strong oral skills.

Strong literacy skills are more highly regarded than oral skills in formal education as evidenced, for instance, by standardized testing, which relies on print as a means of conveying the questions and registering the responses. Since the spread of literacy and school culture, oral skills are secondary, an adjunct to learning rather than central to learning. Good oral skills may be fostered and encouraged in formal education, but students will not succeed without concurrent literacy skills. In Kofi Annan's words, "Literacy is a bridge from misery to hope" (United Nations, 1997).

Yet, celebrating literacy should not lead to a disparagement of oral traditions. Many SLIFE excel at oral skills, whereas few Americans do. Americans are not good at remembering and instead often rely on the written word—whether traditional print forms or digital forms—to bolster memory, whether for grocery lists, to-do lists, speeches, stories, or other tasks (Foer, 2011).

In contrast, SLIFE, with their limited literacy have constantly exercised their brains. They have relied on their minds for many years to learn, remember, and transmit extensive and often complicated information. They are frequently members of cultures where the ability to recite poetry and be a good storyteller is highly prized. Somalians and those from other African cultures, for example, are well-known for their oral literature, oral history, and folk knowledge, transmitted across generations (Bigelow, 2010; Fandrych, 2003). The Kurds in the Middle East (Nykiel-Herbert, 2010) and Mayan and Quechuan cultures in Latin America (Krögel, 2009; Worley, 2013) are a few of the many other cultures that have powerful oral traditions.

Theme 2: Freedom of Movement

> Teacher: *They don't know anything about behaving. They're constantly getting up, wandering around, and looking at what others are doing.*

One difference to consider is that school culture has its own norms of behavior that are distinguished from out-of-school norms. SLIFE are not used to the restrictions on movement we expect of our students, particularly in secondary school. Random moving about is generally frowned upon and students are trained in the early grades to remain seated at their desks for the larger part of the school day, regardless of whether the class is learner- or teacher-centered. When students are allowed to move around in the classroom, it is within specific parameters, such as getting up to find a resource, to change learning centers, or go to another class. SLIFE, however, may not understand that they have to ask the teacher's permission to use the restroom and may just get up and leave class.

In typical U.S. high schools, students sit for 90 percent of their classes, which on any given day, amounts to a significant number of hours that students are expected to be still (Strauss, 2014). We must realize that SLIFE are not students who have been trained from the early grades onward to sit at a desk for most of the day, but that they have had freedom of movement as they went about their daily lives and worked to help support the family or cared for other family members.

For SLIFE who had some prior schooling, there was likely more freedom of movement than in U.S. schools. For one, their schools may have met in the open air or with minimal infrastructure. There may not have been desks so students sat on the floor, in the window sills, or wherever they could find a spot. Schools, particularly those in rural areas, may have only held classes for two to three hours a day, rather than the six to seven hours typical in the U.S.

Theme 3: Seeking Help from Peers

Teacher: *I constantly have to tell them to stop talking to their neighbors when they're supposed to be focused on doing their work.*

Another factor to keep in mind is that most SLIFE are members of collectivistic cultures since more than 70 percent of cultures are closer to the collectivistic end of the continuum than to the individualistic end (Triandis, 1995). As discussed in Myth 2, in collectivistic cultures, people prefer to work together rather than individually. When SLIFE don't know what to do, are confused, or don't understand, they are most likely going to seek help from someone from their group who will be able to help them. And, they will do so when they need it and not necessarily at a time and in ways teachers might deem appropriate. For example, the teacher may be talking and notice that two SLIFE are also talking. The teacher may think these two students are not paying attention when, in reality, the less proficient student is seeking assistance in order to understand and do the work. To take another example, teachers will model an activity and then instruct the students to do the rest on their own. For SLIFE, this may well be another time to seek help from another student who may be seated on the other side of the classroom. From their perspective, they are not disobeying the teacher but doing their best to complete the work by working together and using others as a resource. Thus, the behavior of SLIFE described in the teacher's quote, rather than being "bad" or disrespectful," may indicate that they don't know how to deal with U.S. notions of autonomy and individualism in the classroom.

Theme 4: Hand-Raising

Teacher: *I ask a question, but nobody raises their hand.*

And the flip side of this:

Teacher: *I ask a question, and they all raise their hands even though they don't know the answer.*

SLIFE may not understand the role of raising one's hand in a U.S. classroom (Kusserow, 2004; Marshall & DeCapua; 2013; Mejía-Arauz et al., 2012). Raising one's hand to respond to teachers' questions indicates active involvement (Sahlström, 2002). Students who raise their hands—and correctly respond to the questions— are generally evaluated more favorably by teachers (Howard & Henney, 1998; Takahashi, 2014). (Myth 6 discussed the classroom IRF question-answer discourse routine.) Raising one's hand is part of this interaction pattern that also occurs in other common teacher question-answer patterns. SLIFE, in contrast, may have come from an educational system in which there was no hand-raising in response to teacher questions. If, and when, teachers asked questions, it was their role to choose which students to call on.

For other SLIFE, especially those who have had very little prior schooling, raising their hands is not part of a classroom discourse routine, but a demonstration of involvement. From this viewpoint, it is appropriate always to raise their hands when teachers ask questions because it indicates that they are actively listening to the teacher, not that they know the answer or have anything to contribute.

Theme 5: Homework

> Teacher: *They never do the homework. I give them second chances and they still don't do their work.*

SLIFE may not do their homework for various reasons. For one, the students may not know how to complete the homework assignment and have no one who can help them. What SLIFE are assigned to do is often well beyond their abilities and they are not given the kinds of support they need (Dooley, 2009; Roy & Roxas, 2011). Roxas (2010) describes a case where, after investigating a teacher's complaint that a SLIFE was handing in no homework, he discovered that the student was completely lost and overwhelmed by the requirements for his world literature class. The SLIFE did not have the English proficiency, the literacy skills, or the prior content knowledge. He was being asked, for instance, to read and understand *Beowolf*, yet he was struggling in a beginning ESL course to complete assignments, such as writing "a paragraph in which there were three verbs, three subjects, and one interjection" (p. 523).

Another reason some SLIFE do not do their homework is that they have extensive responsibilities outside of school that are not typical for the average U.S. adolescent. It is not unusual for them to be primary caregivers of younger siblings or older relatives, be responsible for household chores, and hold jobs that contribute significantly to the financial well-being of their family (Martínez, 2009). And those SLIFE who have developed some language proficiency are often responsible for accompanying other family members to health services offices and governmental and service agency appointments in order to translate for them (McBrien, 2005; Yeh et al., 2008). Such responsibilities leave little, if any time, for SLIFE to do homework. While other learners may also have such responsibilities, for SLIFE, given their other challenges, such obligations very much affect their ability to produce the required work for their home assignments.

Finally, the living circumstances of SLIFE may not be conducive to doing homework. SLIFE may live in tight, noisy quarters with numerous family members and have no place, quiet or otherwise, to do homework. Students may not have resources, whether books, computers, internet access, or other resources in their home, and they may not be familiar with or able to use library resources. Their parents or caretakers may spend long hours at work, meaning these young people lack adult supervision that could encourage them to complete homework (Bang, 2012).

Theme 6: Academic Ways of Thinking

> Teacher: *The students don't get what they're supposed to do. I ask them to do worksheets on material we've worked on and they can't do them. Recently, we were doing a geography lesson and the students were supposed to organize the bodies of water into oceans, lakes, and rivers. Why did some of them want to tell me about the lake they grew up by?*

> Teacher: *I provide graphic organizers to help them, but they can't seem to understand how to use them.*

Formal education teaches us to interpret and understand the world in specific ways. Students learn to build and demonstrate knowledge through school-based tasks such as organizing types of bodies of water (DeCapua & Marshall, 2011; Marshall & DeCapua, 2013).

For SLIFE, most of their learning experiences have taken place in the real world. Their way of thinking is based on situational or contextual factors: What is in the lake that we can eat? What grows around the lake that we use? From the perspective of school culture, on the other hand, academic ways of thinking are natural; it makes perfect sense to categorize bodies of water according to type. This is classification, just as we explored earlier in the section on Western-style formal education and academic ways of thinking. It is abstract classification based on shared characteristics determined by an academic (or scientific) way of thinking.

Graphic organizers are typically considered scaffolds to help learners because they visually allow them to see how facts, ideas, or concepts relate to each other. However, graphic organizers are not useful learning aids for those who have not yet developed the tools to interpret them. Recall that Mr. Bisserby tried to use drawings to help his SLIFE understand the reading, but the drawings were not scaffolds for his students because they were two-dimensional representations rather than the real, three-dimensional world they were used to. Graphic organizers are another form of line drawings. While SLIFE are in the process of developing literacy and academic ways of thinking, the graphic organizer itself must be scaffolded. Once students understand the purpose and function of graphic organizers, they can become good learning supports.

These issues illustrate the challenges educators face when with working with SLIFE. Clearly there is a need for an approach that positions educators in a way that success becomes more likely and that teachers like Mr. Bisserby will experience positive results.

Culturally Responsive Teaching

To meet the needs of SLIFE, educators must make a major paradigm shift and implement radically different pedagogy. This pedagogy must be based on the precepts of culturally responsive teaching, which holds that effectively teaching culturally and linguistically diverse students takes place when teachers have in-depth understanding of both their own and their students' cultures (Gay, 2000, 2010). Helaine Marshall and I have developed the Mutually Adaptive Learning Paradigm (MALP®), a culturally responsive instructional approach specifically designed to be implemented with SLIFE. MALP® is culturally responsible because it requires teachers to understand who their learners are and what their preferred learning paradigm is so that they can adapt and incorporate preferred formal educational practices into their teaching. MALP® provides teachers with a framework for understanding what works—and what doesn't—and why. Here is a short summary to introduce this instructional approach. (MALP® is presented and explored thoroughly in DeCapua & Marshall, 2011, and Marshall & DeCapua, 2013.)

MALP® consists of three components: conditions, processes, and activities. The first component, *conditions*, refers to underlying expectations about learning and teaching. The second, *processes*, refers to how learners prefer to access and transmit knowledge and information; the third, *activities*, refers to the types of tasks learners engage in to build and demonstrate mastery. Each group— SLIFE and U.S. educators—prefers opposing conditions, processes, and activities. MALP® is a transitional approach that helps move SLIFE toward the demands and expectations of Western-style formal education by requiring both SLIFE and teachers to change and adapt: Educators accept the conditions SLIFE need to move learning forward; educators combine the preferred processes of SLIFE for learning with those processes essential in formal education; and they assist SLIFE in learning the tasks and academic ways of thinking by carefully scaffolding them with familiar language and content.

For example, one element of *conditions* is relevancy. SLIFE need immediate relevance to their own lives, but formal education is based on future relevance. SLIFE come from prior learning experiences that have occurred in the context of the real world and where what they learn is immediately relevant in the sense that they apply what they learn while they are learning it (Rogoff, 2003). In real-world contexts, you learn to cook to prepare food for your family to eat at that moment. Or, you develop agricultural knowledge while working on a farm or carpentry skills in the process of building something (DeCapua & Marshall, 2011). In formal education, knowledge is separated into discrete subject areas and removed from daily life (Robinson, 2011). Learning is future-oriented and geared toward learning how to learn, and it is not immediately relevant to the real world and life (Bruner, 1966). Once educators appreciate the contrast between these two views of relevancy and the importance of immediate relevance to SLIFE, they can accept this condition and ensure that there is always something of immediate relevance to students in a lesson, which may not be anything related to the lesson content or curriculum.

Let's now look at the second component, *processes*. One element is oral transmission and the written word. For SLIFE, literacy has not been critical in their lives and they prefer the oral mode. In formal education, good literacy skills are essential. Therefore, in developing the literacy skills of SLIFE, we combine the oral with the written, the way it is done in early literacy with young children or emergent literacy for non-literate adults. One example of this is pointing to each word and asking students to do the same as a text is read aloud.

The final component is *activities*. Formal education is based on school-based tasks derived from academic ways of thinking, also referred to as higher-order or complex thinking skills. A popular way of looking at these academic ways of thinking is through Bloom's taxonomy, first proposed in 1958 and later revised by Anderson and Krathwohl (2001) (see Figure 7.3).

The school tasks in which students are expected to engage are all based on academic ways of thinking, as shown in the dogs and rabbits example of characteristics, classification, and defining.

Figure 7.3: Bloom's Revised Taxonomy and Related Verbs

Create	arrange, combine, compose, construct, design, develop, generate, infer, predict
Evaluate	argue, assess, conclude, critique, debate, determine, evaluate, justify, support
Analyze	categorize, classify, compare, contrast, diagram, distinguish, interpret, relate, solve
Apply	apply, calculate, demonstrate, experiment, illustrate, produce, sequence, teach, use
Understand	calculate, discuss, explain, identify, provide examples, recognize, retell
Remember	choose, define, describe, group, label, list, record, repeat, underline

Because academic ways of thinking are school-based, SLIFE cannot be expected to be ready and able to engage in common learning tasks without scaffolding. Teachers of SLIFE must introduce and practice academic ways of thinking and do so separately from content and literacy lessons until the task and the underlying academic way of thinking itself are familiar. Then, teachers can introduce new language and content.

What We Can Do . . .

1. Gain intercultural competence by truly understanding the students.

Learn who your students are beyond the basics such as their names, ages, where they are from, and what language(s) they speak. For example, who are they as people? What have their prior life and/or school experiences been that they would like you to know about? What are their beliefs, norms, values, and funds of knowledge? Use the Intercultural Communication Framework, discussed in depth in DeCapua and Marshall (2011) and Marshall and DeCapua (2013).

In brief, the Intercultural Communication Framework (ICF) consists of three principles:

1. **Develop an ongoing, two-way relationship with your students and their families.** This means not only that you communicate to them about school but also ensure that they have opportunities to communicate to you about who they are, what they expect, and what they need.
2. **Identify priorities in your culture and in theirs.** When you have established a relationship with your students, it becomes easier to understand what their priorities are. These are often significantly different from yours, which have been formed through the lens of formal education. Accommodate their priorities where possible, and transition them to your priorities where necessary.
3. **Make the unfamiliar familiar.** Knowing which associations to make between familiar and unfamiliar material, a core pedagogical practice, becomes successful once you have insights into your students (Principle 1) and their priorities (Principle 2).

2. Raise self-awareness and that of colleagues about SLIFE.

Educating SLIFE is not remedial work or a matter of "dumbing down" content. Avoid looking at SLIFE through a deficit lens. They have developed different ways of understanding and interpreting the world than those valued in formal education. They have abundant funds of knowledge and have had substantial life experiences that are different from the knowledge and practices of schooling.

SLIFE have not had opportunity to learn what is expected and assumed in formal education for their age and grade-level. Teaching SLIFE requires a different mindset and different pedagogy than teaching other learners. To do so requires truly understanding who SLIFE are and what makes their learning paradigm different than the one of formal education:

- When interacting with SLIFE and their families, use the ICF presented in #1.
- Read articles about SLIFE (see the references in this chapter, for instance).
- Watch videos or slide presentations that describe, quote, and/or interview SLIFE. These can be located by searching "students limited / interrupted formal education."

3. Teach SLIFE the culture of school.

Regardless of their age, do not assume that they know the basics of school culture, such as where to write their name on a sheet of paper, when to stand in line, and how to manage and organize notebooks and paper. Here are a few suggestions for helping SLIFE adjust to school. Additional and more detailed suggestions can be found in DeCapua, Smathers, and Tang (2009):

- Do not assume SLIFE can read school maps or room numbers and/or easily follow the numbering or lettering system used in your school. Help newly arrived SLIFE learn where to find classes, offices, the resource center, the cafeteria, restrooms, and the gymnasium. Assign a buddy to escort the students.
- Post schedules prominently. Do not just give SLIFE hard copies. Ask teachers to draw the students' attention to schedules before and after each class, at least until they are very clear about them.
- Develop a simple color code for schedules. Use a variety of colors for the different classes, time periods, and room numbers. For example, make social studies

one color and the room number and period the same color; use another color for the ESL class. By color coding, you make classes, times, and rooms visually obvious, particularly for SLIFE with low literacy, and it helps all SLIFE when classes do not always meet at the same time every day.

- Post a daily class/lesson schedule. (This is in addition to any other schedules.) While this is a standard practice in elementary grades, it is less common in secondary school, yet it is a valuable means for helping SLIFE follow the structure of a lesson.
- Establish classroom routines. Incorporating routines are important to help SLIFE understand what they need to do when and to lessen their frustration of trying to "do school" while learning a new language and new content.
- Teach students explicitly what they need to do. For example, if SLIFE are writing through or well above the lines on lined paper, show them how they should be doing it. Likewise, if they are writing their names randomly on their work, show them where their name belongs. Review any such procedures regularly with SLIFE until they become habits.
- Do not expect SLIFE will remember everything you tell them or do things correctly the first time around. They are learning new classroom behaviors and procedures; you are not remediating what they "should" already know.
- Avoid overloading and overwhelming SLIFE with paper and other print materials. Always keep in mind that SLIFE are learning to become comfortable with print. Evaluate carefully what materials SLIFE really need. Give out worksheets, instructions, letters, and so on judiciously so that there is less for them to organize and keep track of. Be sure that a page does not have too much on it. For lower literacy SLIFE, use large type.

- For SLIFE who are not used to sitting still for long stretches of time, provide in-class opportunities for them to move around. For instance, set up learning stations or centers where different pairs or groups of students work on specific activities for a set amount of time before moving on to another station.
- Ask former SLIFE or those who have been here for a few months to prepare a newcomer booklet of things they found confusing or difficult to share with newly arrived students. These booklets can be very simple, with drawings, photographs, and minimal words, phrases, and basic sentences. They can be expanded and added to as other SLIFE participate and want to include additional information. (See Marshall & DeCapua, 2010, 2013, for more details, suggestions, and sample booklets.)

4. Intentionally implement the Mutually Adaptive Learning Paradigm (MALP®).

Learn about and fully implement the Mutually Adaptive Learning Paradigm or MALP®. This culturally responsive instructional model specifically designed for SLIFE is outlined in the What the Research Says section and extensively explored in DeCapua and Marshall (2011, 2015); Marshall (1998); and Marshall and DeCapua (2013).

Once teachers understand what the MALP® instructional model is and how it works in transitioning SLIFE to the needs and demands of U.S. classrooms, they are encouraged to use the MALP® Teacher Planning Checklist. This Checklist can be used for planning, reflection, and teacher observations. Resources, including books and articles on MALP®, are available at malpeducation. com.

Mutually Adaptive Learning Paradigm®
MALP® Teacher Planning Checklist

A. Accept Conditions for Learning
A1. I am making this lesson/project immediately relevant to my students' lives. How?
A2. I am helping students develop and maintain interconnectedness with each other. How?

B. Combine Processes for Learning
B1. I am incorporating both shared responsibility and individual accountability. How?
B2. I am scaffolding the written word through oral interaction. How?

C. Focus on New Activities for Learning
C1. I am focusing on decontextualized tasks requiring academic ways of thinking. How?
C2. I am making these new tasks accessible with familiar language and content. How?

Adapted from DeCapua, A., & Marshall, H.W. (2011). *Breaking New Ground: Teaching Students with Limited or Interrupted Formal Education in Secondary Schools,* University of Michigan Press, p. 68. Available at malpeducation.com.

References

Adichie, C. (2009, July). The danger of a single story [Video file]. Retrieved from https://www.ted.com/talks/chimamanda_adichie_the_danger_of_a_single_story

Agbenyega, J., & Deku, P. (2011). Building new identities in teacher preparation for inclusive education in Ghana. *Current Issues in Education, 14*, 1–36.

Ahmed, A., & Myhill, D. (2016). The impact of the socio-cultural context on L2 English writing of Egyptian university students. *Learning, Culture and Social Interaction, 11*, 117–129.

Akechi, H., Senju, A., Uibo, H., Kikuchi, Y., Hasegawa, T., & Hietanen, J. (2013). Attention to eye contact in the West and East: Automatic responses and evaluative ratings. *PLOS ONE, 8*, 1–10.

Altinyelken, H. (2012). Pedagogical renewal in sub-Saharan Africa: The case of Uganda. *Comparative Education, 46*, 151–171.

Amachai-Hamburger, Y., Kingsbury, M., & Schneider, B. (2013). Friendship: An old concept with a new meaning? *Computers in Human Behavior, 29*, 33–39.

Andersen, P., Hecht, M., Hoobler, G., & Smallwood, M. (2003). Nonverbal communication across cultures. In W. Gudykunst (Ed.), *Cross-cultural and intercultural communication* (pp. 73–90). Thousand Oaks, CA: Sage.

Anderson, B. B., & Venkatesan, M. (1994). Temporal dimensions of consuming behavior across cultures. In S. Hassan & R. Blackwell (Eds.), *Global marketing, perspectives and cases* (pp. 177–195). Orlando, FL: The Dryden Press.

Anderson, L. W., & Krathwohl, D. R. (Eds.). (2001). *A taxonomy for learning, teaching, and assessing: A revision of Bloom's taxonomy of educational objectives*. Boston: Allyn & Bacon.

Andrews, M. (2016). Three cultural models of teacher inte.action valued by Mexican students at a U.S. high school. *Race, Ethnicity and Education, 19*, 368–388.

Angouri, J. (2010). 'If we know about culture, it will be easier to work with one another': Developing skills for handling corporate meetings with multinational participation. *Language and Intercultural Awareness, 10*, 206–224.

Ardila, J. (2004). Transition relevance places and overlapping in (Spanish-English) conversational etiquette. *Modern Language Review, 99*, 635–650.

Arengo, S. (2016). *Classic tales: Level 1, Peach Boy* (2nd ed.). London: Pearson.

Arevalo, I., So, D., & McNaughton-Cassill, M. (2016). The role of collectivism among Latino American college students. *Journal of Latinos and Education, 15*, 3–11.

Aryee, S. (2005). The work family interface in urban sub-Saharan Africa: A theoretical analysis. In S. Poelmans (Ed.), *Work and family: An international research perspective* (pp. 209–228). Mahwah, NJ: Lawrence Erlbaum.

Atkinson, D. (1999). TESOL and culture. *TESOL Quarterly, 33*, 625–654.

Atkinson, D., & Sohn, J. (2013). Culture from the bottom up. *TESOL Quarterly, 47*, 669–693.

Badger, S., Nelson, L., & McNamara, C. (2006). Perceptions of the transition among Chinese and American emerging adults. *International Journal of Behavioral Development, 30*, 84–93.

Baker, W., & Bricker, H. (2010). The effects of direct and indirect speech acts on native English and ESL speakers' perception of teacher written feedback. *System, 10*, 75–84.

Banaji, M., & Greenwald, A. (2013). *Blindspot: Hidden biases of good people*. New York: Delacorte.

Bang, H. (2012). Promising homework practices: Teachers' perspectives on making homework work for newcomer immigrant students. *The High School Journal, 95*, 3–31.

Bardovi-Harlig, K. (2001). Empirical evidence of the need for instruction in pragmatics. In K. R. Rose & G. Kasper (Eds.), *Pragmatics in language teaching* (pp. 12–32). New York: Cambridge University Press.

Bardovi-Harlig, K. (2012). L2 pragmatic awareness: Evidence from the ESL classroom. *Annual Review of Applied Linguistics, 32,* 206–227.

Bardovi-Harlig, K., & Hartford, B. (Eds.). (2005). *Interlanguage pragmatics: Exploring institutional talk.* Mahwah, NJ: Lawrence Erlbaum.

Barnlund, D., & Yoshioka, M. (1990). Apologies: Japanese and American styles. *International Journal of Intercultural Relations, 14,* 193–206.

Bataineh, R. F., & Bataineh, R. F. (2008). A cross-cultural comparison of apologies by native speakers of American English and Jordanian Arabic. *Journal of Pragmatics, 40,* 792–821.

Beal, C. (1992). Did you have a good weekend? Or why there is no such a thing as a simple question in cross-cultural encounters. *Australian Review of Applied Linguistics, 15,* 23–52.

Beebe, L., & Takahashi, T. (1989). Do you have a bag? Social status and patterned variation in second language acquisition. In S. Gass, C. Madden, D. Preston, & L. Selinker (Eds.), *Variation in second language acquisition: Discourse, pragmatics and communication* (pp.103–125). Clevedon, England: Multilingual Matters.

Beebe, L., Takahashi, T., & Uliss-Weltz, R. (1990). Pragmatic transfer in ESL refusals. In R. Scarcella, E. Andersen, & S. Krashen (Eds.), *On the development of communicative competence in a second language* (pp. 55–73). Boston: Newbury House.

Behera, D., & Pramanik, R. (2012). School children in eastern India: Negotiating time and space. *The Oriental Anthropologist, 12,* 79–95.

Bennett, M. (Ed.). (1998). *Basic concepts of intercultural communication: Selected readings.* Yarmouth, ME: Intercultural Press.

Bigelow, M. (2010). *Mogadishu on the Mississippi: Language, racialized identity, and education in a new land.* New York: Wiley-Blackwell.

Birdwhistell, R. L. (1952). *Introduction to kinesics: An annotation system for analysis of body motion and gesture.* Washington, DC: U.S. Department of State, Foreign Service Institute.

Birdwhistell, R. L. (1970). *Kinesics and context: Essays on body motion communication.* Philadelphia: University of Pennsylvania Press.

Bista, K. (2012). Silence in teaching and learning: Perspectives of a Nepalese graduate student. *College Teaching, 60,* 76–82.

Blum-Kulka, S., House, J., & Kasper, G. (1989). *Cross-cultural pragmatics: Requests and apologies.* Norwood, NJ: Ablex.

Boykin, W., Tyler, K., & Miller, O. (2005). In search of cultural themes and their expressions in the dynamics of classroom life. *Urban Education, 40,* 521–549.

Brisk, M. (2011). Learning English as a second language. In M. Schatz & L. Wilkinson (Eds.), *The education of English language learners* (pp. 152–173). New York: Guilford Press.

Brislin, R., & Kim, E. (2003). Cultural diversity in people's understanding and uses of time. *Applied Psychology: An International Review, 52,* 363–382.

Brown, P., & Levinson, S. (1978). Universals in language usage: Politeness phenomena. In E. Goody (Ed.), *Questions in politeness* (pp. 56–318). Cambridge, England: Cambridge University Press.

Brown, P., & Levinson, S. (1987). *Politeness: Some universals in language usage.* Cambridge, England: Cambridge University Press.

Bruner, J. (1966). *Toward a theory of instruction.* Cambridge, MA: Harvard University Press.

Burger King changes slogan to 'Be Your Way' after four decades of 'Have it Your Way.' (2014, May 14). *New York Daily News.* Retrieved from http://www.nydailynews.com/life-style/eats/burger-king-slogan-article-1.1798278

Burgoon, J., Guerrero, L., & Floyd, K. (2010). *Nonverbal communication*. New York: Routledge.

Byon, A. S. (2004). Sociopragmatic analysis of Korean requests: Pedagogical settings. *Journal of Pragmatics, 36*, 1673–1704.

Byram, M. (1997). *Teaching and assessing intercultural communicative competence*. Clevedon, England: Multilingual Matters.

Byram, M. (2012). Language awareness and (critical) cultural awareness—relationships, comparisons and contrasts. *Language Awareness, 11*, 5–13.

Carbaugh, D. (2005). *Cultures in conversation*. Mahwah, NJ: Lawrence Erlbaum.

Casanave, C. (2017). *Controversies in second language writing: Dilemmas and decisions in research and instruction* (2nd ed.). Ann Arbor: University of Michigan Press.

Cazden, C. (2001). *Classroom discourse: The language of teaching and learning* (2nd ed.). Portsmouth, NH: Heinemann.

Chang, L., Mak, M. C. K., Li, T., Wu, B. P., Chen, B. B., & Lu, H. J. (2011). Cultural adaptations to environmental variability: An evolutionary account of East-West differences. *Educational Psychology Review, 14*, 213–230.

Cheatham, G., & Santos, R. M. (2011). Collaborating with families from diverse cultural and linguistic backgrounds. *Young Children, 66*, 76–82.

Chen, R. (2010). Compliments and compliment response research: A cross-cultural survey. In A. Trosberg (Ed.), *Pragmatics across languages and cultures* (pp. 79–102). New York: Walter de Gruyter.

Chen, R. (2015). Weaving individualism into collectivism: Chinese adults' evolving relationship and family values. *Journal of Comparative Family Studies, 46*, 167–179.

Chen, R., & Yang, D. F. (2010). Responding to compliments in Chinese: Has it changed? *Journal of Pragmatics, 42*, 1951–1963.

Chen, Y. S., Chen, C. Y. D., & Chang, M. H. (2011). American and Chinese complaints: Strategy use from a cross-cultural perspective. *Intercultural Pragmatics, 8*, 253–275.

Cheng, B. (2012). Memorization or discussion: Chinese students' struggle at American academic setting. *Journal of International Education and Leadership, 2.* Retrieved from http://www.jielusa.org/wp-content/uploads/2012/01/memorization_-or_-discussion_Baoyan.pdf

Chentsova-Dutton, Y., & Vaughn, A. (2011). Let me tell you what to do: Cultural differences in advice-giving. *Journal of Cross-Cultural Psychology, 43,* 687–703.

Choi, Y., & Lahey, B. (2006). Testing the model minority stereotype: Youth behaviors across racial and ethnic groups. *Social Service Review, 80,* 419–452.

Cikara, M., & Van Bavel, J. (2014). The neuroscience of intergroup relations: An integrative review. *Perspectives on Psychological Science, 9,* 245–274.

Coates, J. (2014). *Women, men and language: A sociolinguistic account of gender differences in language* (3rd ed.). New York: Routledge.

Cole, M. (2005). Cross-cultural and historical perspectives on the developmental consequences of education. *Human Development, 48,* 195–216.

Comadena, M., Hunt, S., & Simonds, C. (2007). The effects of teacher clarity, nonverbal immediacy, and caring on student motivation, affective and cognitive learning. *Communication Research Reports, 24,* 241–248.

Corder, D., & U-Mackey, A. (2015) Encountering and dealing with difference: Second life and intercultural competence. *Intercultural Education, 26,* 409–424.

Coupland, J. (Ed.). (2000). *Small talk.* Harlow, England: Longman.

Coupland, J. (2003). Small talk: Social functions. *Research on Language and Social Interaction, 36,* 1–6.

Crystal, D. (2012). *English as a global language* (2nd ed.). New York: Cambridge University Press.

Dahl, M. (2010). *Failure to thrive in constructivism: A cross-cultural malady.* Rotterdam, The Netherlands: Sense Publishers.

Damen, L. (1987). *Culture learning: The fifth dimension in the language classroom.* Boston: Addison Wesley.

DeCapua, A. (1998). Pragmatic transfer and cultural stereotyping. *Issues in Applied Linguistics, 9,* 21–36.

DeCapua, A. (2016). Reaching students with limited or interrupted formal education: A culturally responsive approach. *Language and Linguistics Compass, 10,* 225–237.

DeCapua, A. (2017). *Grammar for teachers: A guide to American English for native and non-native speakers* (2ⁿᵈ ed.). Amsterdam: Springer.

DeCapua, A., Berkowitz, D., & Boxer, D. (2006). Women talk revisited: Personal disclosures and alignment development. *Multilingua, 25,* 393–412.

DeCapua, A., & Dunham, J. F. (2007). The pragmatics of advice-giving: Cross-cultural perspectives. *Intercultural Pragmatics, 4,* 319–342.

DeCapua A., & Marshall, H. W. (2011). *Breaking new ground: Teaching students with limited or interrupted formal education in U.S. secondary schools.* Ann Arbor: University of Michigan Press.

DeCapua, A., & Marshall, H. W. (2015). Reframing the conversation about students with limited or interrupted formal education: From achievement gap to cultural dissonance. *NASSP Bulletin, 99,* 356–370.

DeCapua, A., & McDonell, T. (2008). There is more to an iceberg than the tip. In J. Paull (Ed.), *From hip-hop to hyperlinks: Teaching about culture in the composition classroom* (pp. 136–148). Newcastle upon Tyne, England: Cambridge Scholars Publishing.

DeCapua, A., Smathers, W., & Tang, F. (2009). *Meeting the needs of students with limited or interrupted schooling: A guide for educators.* Ann Arbor: University of Michigan Press.

DeCapua, A., & Wintergerst, A. (2016). *Crossing cultures in the language classroom* (Second ed.). Ann Arbor: University of Michigan Press.

Denny, S. (2015, May 2). South Korea's generation gap. *The Diplomat.* Retrieved from http://thediplomat.com/2015/05/south-koreas-generation-gap/

de Souza, M. (2013). A case study of schooling practices at an escuela secundaria in Mexico. *The High School Journal, 96,* 301–320.

Deutscher, G. (2010). *Through the language glass: Why the world looks different in other languages.* New York: Metropolitan Books.

Dewey, J. (1916). *Democracy and education.* New York: Macmillan.

Dibiase, R., & Gunnoe, J. (2004). Gender and cultural differences in touching behavior. *The Journal of Social Psychology, 144,* 49–62.

Di Mare, L. (1990). *Ma* and Japan. *Southern Communication Journal, 55,* 319–328.

Dohrenwend, A. (2002). Serving up the feedback sandwich. *Family Practice Management, 9,* 43–46.

Dooley, K. (2009). Re-thinking pedagogy for middle school students with little, no or severely interrupted schooling. *English Teaching: Practice and Critique, 8,* 5–22.

Doss, D., Henley, R., Gokaraju, B., McElreath, D., Lackey, H., Hong, Q., & Miller, L. (2016). Assessing domestic vs. international student perceptions and attitudes of plagiarism. *Journal of International Students, 6,* 542–565.

Durand, T. (2011). Latina mothers' cultural beliefs about their children, parental roles, and education: Implications for effective and empowering home-school partnerships. *Urban Review, 2,* 255–278.

Eckert, P., & McConnell-Ginet, S. (2003). *Language and gender.* New York: Cambridge University Press.

Eisenstein, M., & Bodman, J. (1986). "I very appreciate": Expressions of gratitude by native and non-native speakers of American English. *Applied Linguistics, 7,* 167–185.

Ekman, P., & Friesen, W. (1969). The repertoire of nonverbal behavior. *Semiotica, 1,* 49–98.

Emily Post Institute. (2011). *Emily Post's etiquette* (18th ed.). New York: William Morrow.

Eslami-Rasekh, Z. (2005). Raising the pragmatic awareness of language learners. *ELT Journal, 59,* 199–208.

Etri, W. (2014). The road to understanding intercultural sensitivity in English language teaching (ELT). Part 1: Pre-existing frames for cultural sensitivity. *Cross-Cultural Communication, 10,* 1–9.

Falicov, C. (2006). Family organization: The safety net of close and extended kin. In R. Smith & R. Montilla (Eds.), *Counseling and family therapy with Latino populations: Strategies that work* (pp. 41–62). New York: Routledge.

Fandrych, I. (2003). Socio-pragmatic and cultural aspects of teaching English for academic purposes in Lesotho. *Southern African Linguistics & Applied Language Studies, 21,* 15–27.

Félix-Brasdefer, J. (2008). *Politeness in Mexico and the United States: A contrastive study of the realization and perception of refusals.* Amsterdam: John Benjamins.

Ferris, D. (2007). Preparing teachers to respond to student writing. *Journal of Second Language Writing, 10,* 161–184.

Ferris, D., & Hedgcock, J. (2013). *Teaching L2 composition: Purpose, process, and practice* (3rd ed.). New York: Taylor & Francis.

Fidalgo-Neto, A., Tornaghi, A., Meirelles, R., Bercot, F., Xavier, L., Castor, M., & Alves, L. (2009). The use of computers in Brazilian primary and secondary schools. *Computers & Education, 53,* 677–685.

Flaitz, J. (2006). *Understanding your refugee and immigrant students: An educational, cultural, and linguistic guide.* Ann Arbor: University of Michigan Press.

Flynn, J. (2007). *What is intelligence?* New York: Cambridge University Press.

Foer, J. (2011). *Moonwalking with Einstein.* New York: Penguin.

Fokkema, T., de Jong, G., & Dykstra, P. (2012). Cross-national differences in older adult loneliness. *Journal of Psychology, 146,* 201–228.

Fong, R. W., & Yuen, M. T. (2016). The role of self-efficacy and connectedness in the academic success of Chinese learners. In R. King & A. Bernardo (Eds.), *The psychology of Asian learners: A festschrift in honor of David Watkins* (pp. 157–168). Singapore: Springer.

Frenz-Belkin, P. (2015). "Teacher! You need to give me back my homework": Assessing students' needs for a pragmatics curriculum in an academic ESL program. In S. Gesuato, F. Bianchi, & W. Cheng (Eds.), *Teaching, learning and investigating pragmatics: Principles, methods and practices* (pp. 33–56). Newcastle upon Tyne, England: Cambridge Scholars Publishing.

Gabor, D. (2011). *How to start a conversation and make friends* (Rev. ed.). New York: Fireside.

Gareis, E. (2000). Intercultural friendship: Five case studies of German students in the USA. *Journal of International Studies, 21*, 67–91.

Gareis, E. (2012). Intercultural friendship: Effects of home and host region. *Journal of International & Intercultural Communication, 5*, 309–328.

Gauvain, M., Beebe, H., & Zhao, S. (2011). Applying the cultural approach to cognitive development. *Journal of Cognition and Development, 12*, 121–133.

Gay, G. (2000) *Culturally responsive teaching: Theory, research and practice.* New York: Teachers College Press.

Gay, G. (2010). *Culturally responsive teaching: Theory, research and practice* (2nd ed.). New York: Teachers College Press.

Gelfand, M., Nishii, L., Holcombe, K., Dyer, N., Ohbuchi, K., & Fukuno, M. (2001). Cultural influences on cognitive representations of conflict: Interpretations of conflict episodes in the United States and Japan. *Journal of Applied Psychology, 86*, 1059–1074.

Georgakopoulos, A., & Guerrero, L. (2010). Student perceptions of teachers' nonverbal and verbal communication: A comparison of best and worst professors across six cultures. *International Education Studies, 3*, 3–17.

Gill-Hopple, K., & Brage-Hudson, D. (2012). *Compadrazgo*: A literature review. *Journal of Transcultural Nursing, 23*, 117–123.

Gillies, R. (2014). Cooperative learning: Developments in research. *International Journal of Educational Psychology, 3*, 125–140.

Gitsaki, C. (2011). *Teaching and learning in the Arab world.* Bern, Switzerland: Peter Lang.

Givvin, K., Herbert, J., Jacobs, J., Hollingsworth, H., & Gallimore, R. (2005). Are there national patterns of teaching? Evidence from the TIMSS 1999 video study. *Comparative Education Review, 49,* 311–342.

Goffman, E. (1972). On face-work: An analysis of ritual elements in social interaction. In J. Laver & S. Hutcheson (Eds.), *Communication in face-to-face interaction* (pp. 319–346). Harmondsworth, England: Penguin.

Golato, A. (2005). *Compliments and compliment responses: Grammatical structure and sequential organization.* Philadelphia: John Benjamins.

González, N., Moll, L., & Amanti, C. (Eds.). (2005). *Funds of knowledge: Theorizing practices in households, communities, and classrooms.* Mahwah, NJ: Lawrence Erlbaum.

Grigorenko, E. (2007). Hitting, missing, and in between: A typology of the impact of western education on the non-western world. *Comparative Education, 43,* 165–186.

Gu, Q., Schweisfurth, M., & Day, C. (2009). Learning and growing in a 'foreign' context: Intercultural experiences of international students. *Compare: A Journal of Comparative and International Education, 40,* 7–23.

Gudykunst, W., & Kim, Y. (2003). *Communicating with strangers: An approach to intercultural communication.* New York: McGraw-Hill.

Gudykunst, W., Ting-Toomey, S., & Chua, E. (1988). *Culture and interpersonal communication.* Thousand Oaks, CA: Sage.

Halgunseth, L., Ispa, J., & Rudy, D. (2006). Parental control in Latino families: An integrated review. *Child Development, 77,* 1282–1297.

Hall, A. (2006). Keeping La Llorona alive in the shadow of Cortés: What an examination of literacy in two Mexican schools can teach U.S. educators. *Bilingual Research Journal, 30,* 385–406.

Hall, E. (1966). *The hidden dimension*. New York: Anchor Books.

Hall, E. (1984). *The silent language*. New York: Doubleday. [Reprint of 1959 edition.]

Hardman, F., Abd-Kadir, J., & Smith, F. (2008). Pedagogical renewal: Improving the quality of classroom interaction in Nigerian primary schools. *International Journal of Education Development, 28,* 55–69.

Harris, S. (2001). Being politically impolite: Extending politeness theory to adversarial political discourse. *Discourse and Society, 12,* 451–472.

Hill, N. E. (2009). Culturally-based world views, family processes, and family-school interactions. In S. L. Christenson & A. L. Reschly (Eds.), *The handbook on school-family partnerships for promoting student competence* (pp. 101–127). New York: Routledge.

Hill, N. E., & Torres, K. (2010). Negotiating the American dream: The paradox of aspirations and achievement among Latino students and engagement between their families and schools. *Journal of Social Issues, 66,* 95–112.

Hillard, A. (2017). Twelve activities for teaching the speech act of complaining to L2 learners. *English Teaching Forum, 55,* 2–13. Retrieved from https://americanenglish.state.gov/files/ae/resource_files/etf_55_1_p01_toc.pdf

Hofstede, G. (1980). *Culture's consequences*. Beverly Hills, CA: Sage.

Hofstede, G. (1986). Cultural differences in teaching and learning. *International Journal of Intercultural Relations, 10,* 301–320.

Hofstede, G., Hofstede, G. J., & Minkov, M. (2010). *Cultures and organizations: Software of the mind—Intercultural cooperation and its importance for survival* (3rd ed.). New York: McGraw-Hill.

Holliday, A. (2011). *Intercultural communication and ideology*. Thousand Oaks, CA: Sage.

Holmes, J., & Stubbe, M. (2015). *Power and politeness in the workplace: A sociolinguistic analysis of talk at work* (2nd ed.). New York: Routledge.

Hos, R. (2014) Caring is not enough: Teachers' enactment of ethical care for adolescent students with limited or interrupted formal education (SLIFE) in a newcomer classroom. *Education and Urban Society, 48,* 1–25.

House, J. (2006). Communicative styles in English and German. *European Journal of English Studies, 10,* 249–267.

House, J. (2012). (Im)politeness in cross-cultural encounters. *Language and Intercultural Communication, 12,* 284–301.

Howard, J., & Henney, A. (1998). Student participation and instructor gender in the mixed-age college classroom. *Journal of Higher Education, 69,* 384–405.

Huang, J., & Brown, K. (2009). Cultural factors affecting Chinese ESL students' academic learning. *Education, 129,* 643–653.

Huang, Q. (2014). *The hybrid tiger: Secrets of the extraordinary success of Asian-American kids.* New York: Prometheus.

Hutchby, I. (2008). Participants' orientations to interruptions, rudeness and other impolite acts in talk-in-interaction. *Journal of Politeness Research, 4,* 221–241.

Huth, T., & Taleghani-Nikzam, C. (2006). How can insights from conversation analysis be directly applied to teaching L2 pragmatics? *Language Teaching Research, 10,* 53–79.

Ibarra, R. (2001). *Beyond affirmative action: Reframing the context of higher education.* Madison: University of Wisconsin Press.

Imada, T. (2012). Individualism and collectivism: A content analysis of textbook stories in the United States and Japan. *Journal of Cross-Cultural Psychology, 43,* 576–591.

Imada, T., & Yussen, S. (2012). Reproduction of cultural values: A cross-cultural examination of stories people create and transmit. *Personality and Social Psychology Bulletin, 38,* 114–128.

Ingram, J., & Elliott, V. (2014). Turn taking and 'wait time' in classroom interactions. *Journal of Pragmatics, 62,* 1–12.

Ishihara, N., & Cohen, A. (2010). *Teaching and learning pragmatics: Where language and culture meet.* New York: Longman Pearson.

Jack, R., Blais, C., Scheepers, C., Schyns, P., & Caldara, R. (2009). Cultural confusions show that facial expressions are not universal. *Current Biology, 19*, 1543–1548.

Jackson, L., & Wang, J. L. (2013). Cultural differences in social networking site use: A comparative study of China and the United States. *Computers in Human Behavior, 29*, 910–921.

Jiménez, R., Smith, P., & Martínez-León, N. (2003). Freedom and form: The language and literacy practices of two Mexican schools. *Reading Research Quarterly, 38*, 488–508.

Jones, S. E., & LeBaron, C. (2002). Research on the relationship between verbal and nonverbal communication: Emerging integrations. *Journal of Communication, 52*, 499–521.

Joyce, B., Weil, M., & Calhoun, E. (2014). *Models of teaching* (9th ed.). New York: Pearson.

Julés, A. (2004). *Gender, participation, and silence in the language classroom: Sh-shushing the girls.* New York: Palgrave Macmillan.

Just, N. (2007). The hamburger method of constructive criticism. Retrieved from http://blogs.helsinki.fi/pirttila/files/2008/08/The-Hamburger-method-of-constructive-criticism.pdf

Kember, D., & Watkins, D. A. (2010). Approaches to learning and teaching by the Chinese. In B. M. Harris (Ed.), *The Oxford handbook of Chinese psychology* (pp. 169–185). New York: Oxford University Press.

Kendon, A. (2004). *Gesture: Visible action as utterance.* New York: Cambridge University Press.

Kilian, S. (2015). *Don't let me be misunderstood: Wie wir weltweit besser verstanden werden – Mit den do's und don'ts der internationalen Kommunikation.* [*How we can be better understood around the world – the do's and don'ts of international communication*]. Munich: Ariston Verlag.

Kim, Y. Y. (2001). *Becoming intercultural: An integrative theory of communication and cross-cultural adaptation.* Thousand Oaks, CA: Sage.

Kim, Y., Sohn, D., & Choi, S. M. (2011). Cultural differences in motivations for using social network sites: A comparative study of American and Korean college students. *Computers in Human Behavior, 27*, 365–372.

Kincheloe, J. (2006). Introducing metropedagogy: Sorry, no short cuts in education. In J. Kinchelow & K. Hayes (Eds.), *Metropedagogy: Power, justice and the urban classroom* (pp. 1–39). Rotterdam, The Netherlands: Sense Publishers.

King, J. (2013). *Silence in the second language classroom.* Basingstoke, England: Palgrave Macmillan.

King, R., McInerney, D., & Watkins, D. (2012). Competitiveness is not that bad…at least in the East: Testing the hierarchical model of achievement motivation in the Asian setting. *International Journal of Intercultural Relations, 36*, 446–457.

Kirch, M. (1979). Non-verbal communication across cultures. *The Modern Language Journal, 63*, 416–424.

Knapp, M., Hall, J. A., & Horgan, T. (2013). *Nonverbal communication in human interactions* (8th ed.). New York: Wadsworth Cengage.

Köhler, T., Cramton, C., & Hinds, P. (2012). The meeting genre across cultures: Insights from three German-American collaborations. *Small Group Research, 43*,159–185.

Kotthoff, H., & Spencer-Oatey, H. (Eds.). (2007). *Handbook of intercultural communication.* Berlin: Walter de Gruyter.

Kramsch, C. (1998a). *Language and culture.* Oxford, England: Oxford University Press.

Kramsch, C. (1998b). The privilege of the intercultural speaker. In M. Byram & M. Flemming (Eds.), *Language learning in intercultural perspective* (pp. 16–31). New York: Cambridge University Press.

Krögel, A. (2009). Dangerous repasts: Food and the supernatural in the Quechua oral tradition. *Food and Foodways, 17*, 104–132.

Kuhn, T. (2012). *The structure of scientific revolutions* (5th ed.). Chicago: University of Chicago Press.

Kusserow, A. (2004). *American individualisms: Child rearing and social class in three neighborhoods.* New York: Palgrave.

Kwon, J. (2004). Expressing refusals in Korean and American English. *Multilingua, 23,* 339–364.

Lambrev, V. (2015). Cultural mismatch in Roma parents' perceptions: The role of culture, language, and traditional Roma values in schools. *Alberta Journal of Educational Research, 61,* 432–448.

Lanteigne, B. (2007). A different culture or just plain rude? *English Teaching: Practice and Critique, 6,* 89–98.

Lapakko, D. (1997). Three cheers for language: A closer examination of a widely cited study of nonverbal communication. *Communication Education, 46,* 63–67.

Lauer, R. (1981). *Temporal man: The meaning and uses of social time.* New York: Praeger.

Lee, S., Turnbull, A., & Zan, F. (2009). Family perspectives: Using a cultural prism to understand families from Asian cultural backgrounds. *Intervention in School and Clinic, 45,* 99–108.

le Roux, J. (2002) Effective educators are culturally competent communicators. *Intercultural Education, 13,* 37–48.

Levine, R. (1997). *A geography of time.* New York: Basic Books.

LeVine, R., & LeVine, S. (2016). *Do parents matter? Why Japanese babies sleep soundly, Mexican siblings don't fight, and American families should just relax.* New York: Public Affairs.

Lewis, R. (2006). *When cultures collide* (3rd ed.). Boston: Nicholas Brealey.

Li, H. (2006). Backchannel responses as misleading feedback in intercultural discourse. *Journal of Intercultural Communication Research, 35,* 99–116.

Li, J. (2012). *Cultural foundations of learning: East and West.* New York: Cambridge University Press.

Li, L., Mazer, J., & Ju, R. (2011). Resolving international teaching assistant language inadequacy through dialogue: Challenges and opportunities for clarity and credibility. *Communication Education, 60,* 461–478.

Limburg, H., & Locher, M. (Eds.). (2012). *Advice in discourse: Pragmatics & beyond.* Amsterdam: John Benjamins.

Louw, K., Derwing, T., & Abbott, M. (2010). Teaching pragmatics to L2 learners for the workplace: The job interview. *The Canadian Modern Language Review, 66,* 739–758.

Lubin, G. (2013, August 29). The most surprising things about America, according to an Indian international student. *Business Life.* Retrieved from http://www.businessinsider.com/the-weirdest-things-about-america-2013-8

Luster, T., Saltarelli, J., Rana, M., Qin, D., Bates, L., & Burdick, K. (2009). The experiences of Sudanese unaccompanied minors in foster care. *Journal of Family Psychology, 21,* 386–395.

Maíz-Arévalo, C. (2012). "Was that a compliment?" Implicit compliments in English and Spanish. *Journal of Pragmatics, 44,* 980–996.

Manes, J. (1983). Compliments: A mirror of cultural values. In N. Wolfson & E. Judd (Eds.), *Sociolinguistics and language acquisition* (pp. 82–95). Rowley, MA: Newbury House.

Mangaliso, M. (2001). Building competitive advantage from ubuntu: Management lessons from South Africa. *Academy of Management Executive, 14,* 23–33.

Marín, G., & VanOss Marín, B. (1991). *Research with Hispanic populations.* Newbury Park, CA: Sage.

Marshall, H. W. (1998). A mutually adaptive learning paradigm (MALP) for Hmong students. *Cultural Circles, 3,* 134–141.

Marshall, H. W., & DeCapua, A. (2010). The newcomer booklet: A project for limited formally schooled students. *ELT Journal, 64,* 396–404.

Marshall, H. W., & DeCapua, A. (2013). *Making the transition to classroom success: Culturally responsive teaching for struggling language learners.* Ann Arbor: University of Michigan Press.

Martínez, I. (2009). What's age gotta do with it? Understanding the age-identities and school-going practices of Mexican immigrant youth in New York City. *The High School Journal, 92,* 34–48.

Matsumoto, D. (2006). Culture and nonverbal behavior. In V. Manusov & M. Patterson (Eds.), *Handbook of nonverbal communication* (pp. 219–235). Thousand Oaks, CA: Sage.

Matsumoto, Y. (1988). Reexamination of the universality of face: Politeness phenomena in Japanese. *Journal of Pragmatics, 38,* 403–426.

Matsumoto, Y. (1989). Politeness and conversational universals—Observations from Japanese. *Journal of Pragmatics, 12,* 403–426.

Maynard, S. (1997). Analyzing interactional management in native/non-native English conversation: A case of listener response. *International Review of Applied Linguistics in Language Teaching, 35,* 37–60.

McBrien, J. L. (2005). Educational needs and barriers for refugee students in the United States: A review of the literature. *Review of Educational Research, 75,* 329–364.

McConachy, T., & Hata, K. (2013). Addressing textbook representations of pragmatics and culture. *ELT Journal, 67,* 294–301.

McDaniel, E., Samovar, L., & Porter, R. (2014). Using intercultural communication: The building blocks. In E. McDaniel, E. Samovar, & R. Porter (Eds.), *Intercultural communication: A reader* (14th ed., pp. 4–18). Boston: Wadsworth.

McGuire, J. (2007). Why has the critical thinking movement not come to Korea? *Asia Pacific Education Review, 8,* 224–232.

McNaught, C. (2012). SoTL at cultural interfaces: Exploring nuance in learning designs at a Chinese University. *International Journal for the Scholarship of Teaching and Learning, 6,* 1–7.

Mehrabian, A., & Ferris, S. (1967). Inference of attitudes from nonverbal communication in two channels. *Journal of Consulting Psychology, 31,* 248–252.

Mehrabian, A., & Wiener, M. (1967). Decoding of inconsistent communications. *Journal of Personality and Social Psychology, 6,* 109–114.

Meihami, H., & Khanlarzadeh, M. (2015). Pragmatic content in global and local ELT textbooks: A micro analysis study. *SAGE Open*, 1–10. Retrieved from http://journals.sagepub.com/doi/abs/10.1177/2158244015615168

Mejía-Arauz, R., Rogoff, B., Daxter, A., & Najafi, B. (2007). Cultural variation in children's social organization. *Child Development, 78*, 1001–1014.

Meyer, E. (2014). *Culture map: Breaking through the invisible boundaries of global business*. New York: Public Affairs.

Mintner, A. (2016, May 16). Why China doesn't care about privacy. [Blog post]. Retrieved from https://origin-www.bloombergview.com/articles/2016-05-17/why-china-doesn-t-care-about-privacy/

Mirivel, J., & Tracy, K. (2005). Premeeting talk: An organisationally crucial form of talk. *Research on Language and Social Interaction, 38*, 1–34.

Moran, R., Abramson, N., & Moran, S. (2014). *Managing cultural differences* (8th ed.). New York: Routledge.

Moreno-Cabrera, J. (2011). Speech and gesture: An integrational approach. *Language Sciences, 33*, 615–622.

Morkus, N. (2014). Refusals in Egyptian Arabic and American English. *Journal of Pragmatics, 70*, 86–107.

Mott-Smith, J. A., Tomaš, Z., & Kostka, I. (2017). *Teaching effective source use: Classroom approaches that work*. Ann Arbor: University of Michigan Press.

Mundava, M., & Chaudhuri, J. (2007). Understanding plagiarism: The role of librarians at the University of Tennessee in assisting students to practice fair use of information. *College and Research Libraries News, 68*, 1–5.

Murphy, B., & Neu, J. (1996). My grade's too low: The speech act set of complaining. In S. M. Gass & J. Neu (Eds.), *Speech acts across cultures: Challenges to communication in a second language* (pp. 191–216). Berlin: Walter de Gruyter.

Nakane, I. (2005). Negotiating silence and speech in the classroom. *Multilingua, 24,* 75–100.

Nasir, N., & Hand, V. (2006). Exploring sociocultural perspectives on race, culture and learning. *Review of Educational Research, 76,* 449–475.

Ngo, B. (2010). Doing "diversity" at Dynamic High: Problems and possibilities of multicultural education in practice. *Education and Urban Society, 42,* 473–495.

Ngware, M., Mutisya, M., & Oketch, M. (2012). Patterns of teaching style and active teaching: Do they differ across subjects in low and high performing primary schools in Kenya? *London Review of Education, 10,* 35–54.

Nhung, P. T. H. (2014). Strategies employed by the Vietnamese to respond to compliments and the influence of compliment receivers' perception of the compliment on their responses. *International Journal of Linguistics, 6,* 142–165.

Northouse, P. (2007). *Leadership: Theory and practice* (4th ed.). Thousand Oaks, CA: Sage.

Norton, B. (2001). Non-participation, imagined communities and the language classroom. In M. Breen (Ed.), *Learner contributions to language learning* (pp. 159–171). New York: Pearson.

Nydell, M. (2012). *Understanding Arabs: A contemporary guide to Arab society* (5th ed.). Boston: Nicholas Brealey.

Nykiel-Herbert, B. (2010). Iraqi refugee students: From a collection of aliens to a community of learners—the role of cultural factors in the acquisition of literacy by Iraqi refugee students with interrupted formal education. *Multicultural Education, 17,* 2–14.

Oberg, K. (1960). Culture shock: Adjustment to a new cultural environment. *Practical Anthropology, 7,* 177–182.

Ordoñez-Jasis, R., Dunsmore, K. L., Herrera, G., Ochoa, C., Diaz, L., & Zuniga-Rios, E. (2016). Communities of caring: Developing curriculum that engages Latino/a students' diverse literacy practices. *Journal of Latinos and Education, 15,* 333–343.

Orton, J. (2006). Responses to Chinese speakers of English. *International Review of Applied Linguistics in Language Teaching, 44*, 287–309.

Oyserman, D., & Lee, S. (2008). Does culture influence what and how we think? Effects of priming individualism and collectivism. *Psychological Bulletin, 134*, 311–342.

Özdemir, Ç., & Rezvani, S. A. (2010). Interlanguage pragmatics in action: Use of expressions of gratitude. *Procedia—Social and Behavioral Sciences, 3*, 194–202.

Pai, Y., Adler, S., & Shadlow, L. (2006). *Cultural foundations of education* (4th ed.). Upper Saddle River, NJ: Merrill/Prentice Hall.

Pan, Y. (2012). Facework in refusals in Chinese survey interviews. *Journal of Politeness Research, 8*, 53–74.

Paradise, R., & Rogoff, B. (2009). Side by side: Learning by observing and pitching in. *Ethos, 37*, 102–138.

Park, H. S., & Lee, H. E. (2012). Cultural differences in "thank you." *Journal of Language and Social Psychology, 31*, 138–156.

Patterson, M. (1990). Functions of non-verbal behavior in social interaction. In H. Giles & W. Robinson (Eds.), *Handbook of language and social psychology* (pp. 101–118). New York: Wiley and Son.

Peeples, J., Hall, B. J., & Seiter, J. (2012). The flipper debate: Teaching intercultural communication through simulated conflict. *Communication Teacher, 26*, 87–91.

Peterson, B. (2004). *Cultural intelligence.* Yarmouth, ME: Nicholas Brealey.

Pinto, D., & Raschio, R. (2007). A comparative study of requests in heritage speaker Spanish, L1 Spanish and L1 English. *International Journal of Bilingualism, 11*, 135–155.

Ponzetti, J., & James, J. (2003). *International encyclopedia of marriage and family* (Vol. 1, 2nd ed.). Gale, NY: MacMillan Reference.

Prelutsky, J. (2008). *My parents think I'm sleeping (I can read level 3).* New York: HarperCollins.

Price, P. J. (1997). *Open sesame: Understanding American English and culture through folktales and stories*. Ann Arbor: University of Michigan Press.

Prowse, J., & Goddard, J. (2010). Teaching across cultures: Canada and Qatar. *Canadian Journal of Higher Education, 40*, 119–134.

Purcell-Gates, V., Lenters, K., McTavish, M., & Anderson, J. (2014, spring/summer). Working with different cultural patterns and beliefs: Teachers and families learning together. *Multicultural Education, 21*, 17–22.

Qin, X. (2014). Teaching foreign language by exploring intercultural misunderstanding. *Intercultural Communication, 3*, 66–82.

Ramirez, A. Y. F. (2003). Dismay and disappointment: Parental involvement of Latino immigrant parents. *Urban Review, 35*, 93–110.

Reid, J. (Ed.). (2008). *Writing myths: Applying second language research to classroom teaching*. Ann Arbor: University of Michigan Press.

Reinke, W., Lewis-Palmer, T., & Martin, E. (2007). The effect of visual performance feedback on teacher behavior-specific praise. *Behavior Modification, 31*, 247–263.

Reiter, R. M. (2002). A contrastive study of conventional indirectness in Spanish: Evidence from Peninsular and Uruguayan Spanish. *Pragmatics, 12*, 135–151.

Ren, W., & Zheng, H. (2016). The representation of pragmatic knowledge in recent ELT textbooks. *ELT Journal 70*, 424–434.

Renee, E., Brock, B., Frost, J., Harvey A., & Navarro, M. (2017). That's not what I meant: How misunderstanding is related to channel and perspective-taking. *Journal of Language and Social Psychology, 36*, 188–210.

Richmond, Y., & Gestrin, P. (2009). *Into Africa: A guide to sub-Saharan culture and diversity* (2nd ed.). Boston: Intercultural Press.

Ríos-Águilar, C., & Kiyama, J. (2012). Funds of knowledge: An approach to studying Latina(o) students' transition to college. *Journal of Latino and Education, 11*, 2–16.

Robinson, K. (2011). *Out of our minds: Learning to be creative.* New York: John Wiley & Sons.

Rogoff, B. (2003). *The cultural nature of human development.* New York: Oxford University Press.

Rose, K., & Kasper, G. (2001). *Pragmatics in language teaching.* New York: Cambridge University Press.

Rothstein-Fisch, C., & Trumbull, E. (2008). *Managing diverse classrooms: How to build on students' cultural strengths.* Alexandria, VA: ASCD.

Roxas, K. (2010). Tales from the front line: Teachers responses to Somali Bantu refugee students. *Urban Education, 46,* 513–548.

Roy, L., & Roxas, K. (2011). Exploring counter-stories of Somali Bantu refugees: Experiences in "doing school." *Harvard Educational Review, 81,* 521–542.

Ruby, M., Falk, C., Heine, S., Villa, C., & Silberstein, O. (2012). Not all collectivisms are equal: Opposing preferences for ideal affect between East Asians and Mexicans. *Emotion, 12,* 1206–1209.

Ruxin, J. (2013). *A thousand hills to heaven.* Boston: Little, Brown and Company.

Safadi, M., & Valentine, C. A. (1988). Emblematic gestures among Hebrew speakers in Israel. *International Journal of Intercultural Relations, 4,* 327–361.

Sahlström, F. (2002). The interactional organization of hand raising in classroom interaction. *Journal of Classroom Interaction, 37,* 47–57.

Samarah, A. Y. (2015). Politeness in Arabic culture. *Theory and Practice in Language Studies, 5,* 2005–2016.

Samovar, L., Porter, R., & McDaniel, E. (2012). *Communication between cultures* (8th ed.). Boston: Cengage.

Santagata, R. (2004). "Are you joking or are you sleeping?" Cultural beliefs and practices in Italian and U.S. teachers' mistake-handling strategies. *Linguistics and Education, 15,* 141–164.

Scollon, C. N., Diener, E., Oishi, S., & Biswas-Diener, R. (2004). Emotions across cultures and methods. *Journal of Cross-Cultural Psychology, 35,* 304–326.

Semnani-Azad, Z., & Adair, W. (2011). The display of "dominant" nonverbal cues in negotiation: The role of culture and gender. *International Negotiation, 16,* 451–479.

Shapiro, S., Farrelly, R., & Tomaš, Z. (2014). *Fostering international student success in higher education.* Alexandria, VA: TESOL.

Sharifian M., & Jamarani, M. (2011). Cultural schemas in intercultural communication: A study of the Persian cultural schema of sharmandegi 'being ashamed.' *Intercultural Pragmatics, 8,* 227–251.

Shepard, H. (2014). Culture and cognition: A process account of culture. *Sociological Forum, 29,* 1007–1011.

Shoorman, D., & Velouse, J. J. (2003). Project CASAS: Facilitating the adaptation of recent immigrant students through complex community-wide efforts. *Equity and Excellence in Education, 36,* 308–316.

Slavin, R. (2011). Instruction based on cooperative learning. In R. Mayer & P. Alexander (Eds.), *Handbook of research on learning and instruction* (pp. 344–360). New York: Taylor & Francis.

Smith, J., & Hu, R. (2013). Rethinking teacher education: Synchronizing Eastern and Western views of teaching and learning to promote 21st century skills and global perspectives. *Education Research and Perspectives, 40,* 86–108.

Soudek, M., & Soudek, L. (1985). Non-verbal channels in language learning. *ELT Journal, 39,* 109–114.

Staples, S., Kang, O., & Wittner, E. (2014). Considering interlocutors in university discourse communities: Impacting U.S. undergraduates' perceptions of ITAs through a structured contact program. *English for Specific Purposes, 35,* 54–65.

Steidel, A., & Contreras, J. (2003). A new familism scale for use with Latino populations. *Hispanic Journal of Behavioral Sciences, 25,* 312–330.

Stivers, T., Enfield, N., Brown, P., Englert, C., Hayashi, M., Heinemann, T., Hoymann, G., Rossano, F., de Ruiter, J., Yoon, K. E., & Levinson, S. (2009). Universals and cultural variation in turn-taking conversation. *National Proceedings of the National Academy of Sciences, 106*, 10587–10592.

Strauss, V. (2014, October 24). Teacher spends two days as a student and is shocked at what she learns. *The Washington Post*. Retrieved from https://www.washingtonpost.com/news/answer-sheet/wp/2014/10/24/teacher-spends-two-days-as-a-student-and-is-shocked-at-what-she-learned/?utm_term=.14cbf2b836b2

Taguchi, N. (2011). Teaching pragmatics: Trends and issues. *Annual Review of Applied Linguistics, 31*, 289–310.

Taguchi, N. (2015). Instructed pragmatics at a glance: Where instructional studies were, are, and should be going. *Language Teaching, 48*, 1–50.

Takahashi, J. (2014). Contribution with hand-raising in graduate student self-selection: Bringing legitimacy to the focal shift of talk. *Teachers College, Columbia University Working Papers in TESOL & Applied Linguistics, 16*, 35–39.

Tamis-LeMonda, C., Way, N., Hughes, D., Yoshikawa, H., Kalman, R., & Niwa, E. (2008). Parents' goals for children: The dynamic coexistence of individualism and collectivism in cultures and individuals. *Social Development, 17*, 183–209.

Tangie, K. N. (2015). *Improving learning in secondary schools: Conditions for successful provision and uptake of assessment feedback*. Newcastle upon Tyne, England: Cambridge Scholars Publishing.

Tannen, D. (2005). *Conversational style: Analyzing talk among friends* (Rev. ed.). New York: Oxford University Press.

Tatar, S. (2005). Why keep silent? The classroom participation experiences of non-native English-speaking students. *Language and Intercultural Communication, 5*, 284–293.

TESOL Quarterly submission guidelines. (n.d.). Retrieved from http://onlinelibrary.wiley.com/journal/10.1002/(ISSN)1545-7249/homepage/ForAuthors.html

Thomas, J. (1983). Cross-cultural pragmatic failure. *Applied Linguistics, 4,* 91–112.

Ting-Toomey, S., & Chung, L. (2011). *Understanding intercultural communication* (2nd ed.). New York: Oxford University Press.

Triandis, H. (1995). *Individualism and collectivism.* Boulder, CO: Westview Press.

Trosberg, A. (Ed.). (2010). *Pragmatics across languages and cultures.* New York: Walter de Gruyter.

Trumbull, E., Greenfield, P., Rothstein-Fisch, C., & Quiroz, B. (2007). Bridging cultures in parent conferences: Implications for school psychology. In G. Esquivel, E. Lopez, & S. Nahari (Eds.), *Handbook of multicultural school psychology: An interdisciplinary approach* (pp. 615–636). Mahwah, NJ: Lawrence Erlbaum.

Trytten, D., Lowe, A., & Walden, S. (2012). "Asians are good at math. What an awful stereotype": The model minority stereotype's impact on Asian American engineering students. *Journal of Education, 101,* 439–468.

United Nations. (1997, September 4). Secretary-General [Kofi Annan] stresses need for political will and resources to meet challenge of fight against illiteracy [Press release]. Retrieved from http://www.un.org/press/en/1997/19970904.SGSM6316.html

Uy, P. S. (2015). Supporting Southeast Asian American family and community engagement for educational success. *Journal of Southeast Asian American Education and Advancement, 10,* 1–17. Retrieved from http://docs.lib.purdue.edu/cgi/viewcontent.cgi?article=1131&context=jsaaea

Vásquez, C., & Fioramonte, A. (2011). Integrating pragmatics into the MA-TESL program: Perspectives from former students. *TESOL-EJ, 15,* 1–22.

Vygotsky, L. (1978). *Mind in society: The development of higher psychological processes.* Cambridge, MA: Harvard University Press.

Wallace, D. F. (2005). Commencement speech at Kenyon College. Retrieved from https://www.theguardian.com/books/2008/sep/20/fiction

Walsh, J., & Sattes, B. (2016). *Quality questioning: Research-based practice to engage every learner.* Thousand Oaks, CA: Corwin.

Ward, C., Bochner, S., & Furnham, A. (2005). *The psychology of culture shock.* New York: Routledge.

Watkins, D. (2000). Learning and teaching: A cross-cultural perspective. *School Leadership and Management, 20,* 161–173.

Watson, J. (2006). *Golden arches east: McDonald's in East Asia* (2nd ed.). Stanford, CA: Stanford University Press.

Weed, J. (2016, November 28). How tour guides abroad learn to cater to exotic Americans. *New York Times.* Retrieved from http://www.nytimes.com

West, C., & Zimmerman, D. (1983). Small insults: A study of interruptions in cross-sex conversations between unacquainted persons. In B. Thorne, C. Kramarae, & N. Henley (Eds.), *Language, gender and society* (pp. 103–117). Rowley, MA: Newbury House.

White, L., Valk, R., & Dialmy, A. (2011). What is the meaning of "on time"? The sociocultural nature of punctuality. *Journal of Cross-Cultural Psychology, 42,* 482–493.

Whitrow, G. (2004). *What is time? The classic account of the nature of time.* New York: Oxford University Press.

Whorf, B. (1956). *Language, thought, and reality: Selected writings of Benjamin Lee Whorf.* Cambridge: MIT Press.

Witte, A. (2011). On the teachability and learnability of intercultural competence: Developing facets of the "inter." In A. Witte & T. Harden (Eds.), *Intercultural competence: Concepts, challenges, evaluations* (pp. 89–108). Oxford, England: Peter Lang.

Witte, A. (2014). *Blending spaces: Mediating and assessing intercultural competence in the L2 classroom.* Berlin: Walter de Gruyter.

Wolfson, N. (1981). Compliments in cross-cultural perspective. *TESOL Quarterly, 15*, 117–124.

Wolfson, N. (1989). *Perspectives: Sociolinguistics and TESOL*. New York: Newbury House.

Woolley, M., Kol, K., & Bowne, G. (2008). The social context of school success for Latino middle school students: Direct and indirect influences of teachers, family, and friends. *The Journal of Early Adolescence, 29*, 43–70.

Worley, P. (2013). *Telling and being told: Storytelling and cultural control in contemporary Yucatec Maya literatures*. Tucson: University of Arizona Press.

Yeh, C., Okubo, Y., Ma, P. W. W., Shea, M., Ou, D., & Pitue, S. (2008). Chinese immigrant high school students' cultural interactions, acculturation, family obligations, language use, and social support. *Adolescence, 43*, 775–790.

Yin, H., Lee, J. C. K., & Wang, W. (2014). Dilemmas of leading national curriculum reform in a global era: A Chinese perspective. *Educational Management Administration & Leadership, 42*, 293–311.

Yin, J. (2013). Popular culture and public imagery: Disney versus Chinese stories of *Mulan*. In M. K. Asante, Y. Miike, & J. Yin (Eds.), *The global intercultural communication reader* (pp. 285–303). New York: Routledge.

Yngve, V. (1970). On getting a word in edgewise. *Papers from the Sixth Regional Meeting of the Chicago Linguistic Society*, 567–578.

Yoon, K. J. (2005). Not just words: Korean social models and the use of honorifics. *Intercultural Pragmatics, 1*, 189–210.

Yu, K. A. (2011). Culture-specific concepts of politeness: Indirectness and politeness in English, Hebrew, and Korean requests. *Intercultural Pragmatics, 8*, 385–409.

Yu, M. C. (2005). Sociolinguistic competence in the complimenting act of native Chinese and American speakers: A mirror of cultural value. *Language and Speech, 48*, 91–119.

Yudkin, D., Rothmund, T., Twardawski, M., Thalia, N., & Van Bavel, J. (2016). Reflexive intergroup bias in third-party punishment. *Journal of Experimental Psychology: General, 145,* 1448–1459.

Yuki, M., Maddux, W., & Masuda, T. (2007). Are the windows to the soul the same in the East and West? Cultural differences in using the eyes and mouth as cues to recognize emotions in Japan and the United States. *Journal of Experimental Social Psychology, 43,* 303–311.

Zarrinabadi, N. (2014). Communicating in a second language: Investigating the effect of teacher on learners' willingness to communicate. *System, 42,* 288–295.

Zhang, Q., & Oetzel, J. (2006). Constructing and validating a teacher immediacy scale: Chinese perspective. *Communication Education, 55,* 218–241.

Zheng, X. (2010). Re-interpreting silence: Chinese international students' verbal participation in U.S. universities. *The International Journal of Learning, 17,* 1447–9494.

Zulfikar, T. (2013). Looking from within: Prospects and challenges for progressive education in Indonesia. *International Journal of Progressive Education, 9,* 124–136.

Zupnik, J. J. (2000). Conversational interruptions in Israeli-Palestinian 'dialogue' events. *Discourse Studies, 2,* 85–110.

Index

advice, giving, 96, 97
apologizing, 96, 97, 101, 102

backchannel cues, 59
Bloom's taxonomy, 149–150
body language. *See* non-verbal
    communication

classification, 139–140, 147, 150
class participation, 108, 119–122;
    in cooperative learning
    approach, 111–112, 113, 116–
    117, 119–120; encouraging,
    125–129; gender variable, 63,
    121; inhibitions, 120–121;
    by students from collectivist
    cultures, 48, 49; in teacher-
    centered learning cultures,
    110, 112, 117, 120
collectivist cultures, 35–51;
    collectivism defined, 4, 39;
    continuum of, 42; curriculum
    in, 45–46; family importance
    in, 13, 37, 39–40, 42, 44–47,
    115; folktales illustrating,
    44–46, 48–49, 50–51; private/
    public sphere and, 58;
    restaurant behavior, 43–44;
    SLIFE and, 143–144; teaching
    styles and, 115–117. *See also*
    individualist cultures
competitiveness, 115
complaining, 43, 78, 89, 93, 97,
    102, 127
compliments, 55, 97, 104

conformity, 37, 43
Confucian tradition, 42–43, 112,
    114, 116
constructivism, 113–114
contact behaviors, 78–79
conversational routines, 93–95
conversational skills, 5, 52–68;
    appropriate topics, 55–58,
    66–67, 94; backchannel cues,
    59; choreography of, 58–62;
    encouraging observation,
    65; gender variable, 63, 121;
    pause length and talk amount,
    59–63, 80, 121; small talk,
    52–58, 63–64; sociocultural
    norms governing, 52–54;
    structured practice, 64. *See also*
    non-verbal communication;
    pragmatics (conversation style)
cooperative learning approach,
    109–114, 116–117, 119–120.
    See also teaching styles
critical incidents for pedagogical
    purposes, 31–32, 49, 66–67,
    104–105, 127
cross-cultural awareness/
    communication, 2–3, 5–7,
    9, 12–13, 27–29, 59, 63, 78,
    84, 96–99, 105–106. *See also*
    stereotypes
*Crossing Cultures in the Language
    Classroom (Second Edition)*
    (DeCapua and Wintergerst), 5
culturally responsive teaching,
    147–155